Translation Theories, Strategies And Basic Theoretical Issues

Prof. A. B. As-Safi
Petra University

The Hashemite Kingdom of Jordan
The Deposit Number At The
National Library
(1675/4/2011)

428
.As- Safi,A.B
Translation Theories Strategies and Basic Theoretical
Issues / A.B. As - Safi.- Amman: Dar Amwaj,2011
Deposit No.: 2011/4/1675
Descriptors: Translation//Linguistics//English Language

ISBN   978-9957-528-16-4

دار أمواج للطباعة والنشر والتوزيع
عمان - الأردن - ماركا الشمالية
تلفاكس: 009624889651 ص.ب: 330959 الأردن 11134
E-mail: amwajpub@yahoo.com

Contents

To my beloved wife,
Rajaa

Preface

It is perhaps axiomatic to say that translation is as old as language, for the different language communities render translation mandatory for their interaction. With translation as an indispensable activity there emerged diverse theories and theoretical reflections to guide it. This diversity stems from the diverse perspectives and approaches to translation with the corollary of a plethora of definitions, types and theories scanned in the first three chapters of Part One. Historically, translation theories began with the Romans, but they have undergone four periods as proposed by George Steiner and surveyed in Chapter Two. Chapter Three furnishes a plethora of ancient and recent theories and models generated from these theories. Chapter Four is devoted to translation/interpreting strategies and their application in English/Arabic translations. Part Two tackles certain basic relevant issues such as translation equivalence, loss and gain, determinacy and indeterminacy, and modalization and lexicalization in Arabic – English translation.

It is sincerely hoped that the students and others specialized or interested in translation will benefit from the present book, the writing of which has actually been motivated by MA students in the postgraduate translation programme at Petra University. To them, I would like to express my profound appreciation.

Part One

Preliminaries, Theories & Strategies

[Prof. A. B. As-Safi]

Chapter One

Preliminaries: Definitions and Types

1.1. Translation: Definitions

There has been a plethora of definitions which E. Nida (1964: 161-164) has elaborately surveyed . He rightly elucidates:

> Definitions of proper translating are almost as numerous and varied as the persons who have undertaken to discuss the subject. This diversity is in a sense quite understandable; for there are vast differences in the materials translated, in the purpose of the publication, and in the needs of the prospective audience (161).

Nevertheless, a definition which is not confined to the mere transference of meaning is furnished by Nida and Taber (1969: 12) who postulate

> Translation consists in reproducing in the receptor language the closest natural equivalent of the source language message, first in terms of **meaning** and

secondly in terms of **style.**
(Emphasis is mine).

Bell (1991: 5-6) seems to have pursued the same line of emphasis on meaning and style in his translation of the definition given by the French theorist, Dubois (1974) :

> Translation is the expression in another language (or the target language) of what has been expressed in another, source language, preserving semantic and stylistic equivalences.

The above definitions also stress the significance of 'equivalence' which underlies the following definitions, among others: given by Meetham and Hudson (1972) and Catford (1965):

> Translation is the replacement of a text in one language by a replacement of an equivalent text in a second language.
> (Meetham and Hudson, 1972: 713)
> Translation is the replacement of textual material in one language (SL) by equivalent textual material in another language (TL).
> (Catford, 1965: 20)

On the other hand, functionalists view translation differently:

> Translation is the production
> of a functional target text
> maintaining a relationship with
> a given source text that is
> specified according to the
> intended or demanded
> function of the target text.

(Nord, in shutttleworth and Cowie, 2007:

182)

Nord, however, distinguishes between two senses of translation: wide and narrow.

> Translation is, in a narrow sense,
> any translational action where a
> source text is transferred into a
> target culture and language.
> According to the form and
> presentation of the source text
> and to the correctibility of the
> target text we distinguish
> between oral translation (=
> 'interpreting') and written
> translation (= 'translation' in the
> narrow sense).
>
> (Nord, 2007: 141)

Widening the above definitions, Sager maintains that translation should reflect the environment in which the professional translation activity takes place:

> Translation is an extremely motivated industrial activity, supported by information technology, which is diversified in response to the particular needs of this form of communication.
>
> (Sager, 1994: 293)

In a similar vein, Koller describes translation as a 'text-processing activity and simultaneously highlights the significance of 'equivalence':

> Translation can be understood as the result of a text-processing activity, by means of which a source-language text is transposed into a target-language text.. Between the resulting text in L2 (the target-language text) and the source text L1 (the source-language text) there exists a relationship which can be designated as translational, or equivalence relation.
>
> (Koller, 1995: 196)

Amongst the above definitions, Nida and Taber's may serve as a basis for our concept of translation as a TL product which is as semantically accurate, grammatically correct, stylistically effective and textually coherent as the SL text. In other words, the translator's main attention should not be focused only on the accurate semantic transference of SL message into the TL, but also on the appropriate syntax and diction in the TL, which are explicitly the translator's (not the source author's) domain of activity which displays his true competence. Indeed, according to Wilss (1969:95), "the notion of translation competence," "is aptly assessed in transfer situations that require at least some degree of adaptation to new and challenging textual demands." He describes such situations as "accommodatory situations" which need "structural adjustment" (ibid) and generally textual manipulation. In point of fact, the competent translator performs multiple tasks with inevitable intricacies of performance. His approach to translating expressive, emotive or expository texts in particular is deemed to be creativity-oriented, that is, hermeneutic/manipulation rather than routine-oriented. In the latter approach, SL words are mechanically replaced by their TL equivalents, albeit one-to-one equivalence rarely, if ever, exists between languages, as will be explicated in Chapter Five below.

1.2. Types

There has also been a plethora of classifications of types of translation albeit the basically overlapping and polarized dichotomy in binary oppositions starting with the oldest 'literal' vs (versus) 'free'. Others subsume 'literary' vs 'non-literary', semantic vs communicative, static vs dynamic, among others. The first type of the afore-mentioned pairs concerns the closeness , sometimes referred to as fidelity or faithfulness to the ST (source text). This type tends to emphasize the inseparability of form from content. The second type deems the source message conveyable in a different form.

The above pairs are classified according to the criterion of method or approach. Two criteria of classification will be elaborated below, namely: code and mode.

1.2.1. Translation Types according to Code

Roman Jakobson (1959 in Schulte and Biguenet, 1992:145) distinguishes three ways of interpreting a verbal sign: it may be translated into other signs of the same language, into another language, or into another code that is nonverbal system of symbols. These three types are succinctly put as follows:

1. Intralingual translation or *rewording* : It is an interpretation of verbal signs by means of other signs of the same language.

2. Interlingual translation or *translation proper* : It is an interpretation of verbal signs by means of some other language.

3. **Intersemiotic translation** or *transmutation* : It is an interpretation of verbal signs by means of signs of nonverbal sign system.

The first type is exemplified by synonyms in the same linguistic code or language, paraphrase or replacing an idiom such as 'pass away' by 'die'. The second type is seen in replacing certain code-units in SL by equivalent code-units in TL. The third refers to the use of signs or signals for the purpose of communication; the most important semiotic system is human language in contrast to other systems such as sign language and traffic signals. Obviously, this type lies within Jakobson's framework in which translation is perceived as the conversion of a sign into another alternative or equivalent sign, be it verbal or nonverbal. (Ibid, 232; and Shuttleworth and Cowie, 2007: 85).

1.2.2. Translation Types according to Mode: Written vs. Oral: Translating/Interpreting: General Remarks

Nida and Taber's above definition, which may best accommodate interpreting as the reproduction of " the closest natural equivalent" of the SL message in the TL", serves as a common ground or interface of translating and interpreting; the former is not mainly or exclusively concerned with the accurate, semantic transference. The translated text should, at least ideally and theoretically, be as semantically accurate, grammatically correct, stylistically effective and textually coherent as the source text.

On the other hand, we may analogously postulate the following workable definition for interpreting:

> Interpreting consists in conveying to the target language the most accurate, natural equivalent of the source language oral message

1.2.2.1. Convergent/Divergent Requirements for Translating/ Interpreting Competence

There are at least five common or interfacial requirements for both translating and interpreting competence vis-à-vis ten for interpreting. The five requirements for competent translators are: mastery or proficiency of SL and TL, thorough knowledge of source and target cultures, familiarity with the topic/register, vocabulary wealth, and finally awareness of the three–phase process, i.e., SL decoding, transcoding or SL-TL transfer and TL encoding. Interpreting, on the other hand, requires at least five more: short-term memory for storage and retrieval, acquaintance with prosodic features and different accents, quick wittedness and full attention, knowledge of short-hand writing for consecutive interpreting and finally self-composure.

1.2.2.2. Translating/Interpreting Constraints

The constraints imposed on the interpreters are more and greater than those on the translator. They also vary in type and degree of intensity as regards the direction of translating or interpreting, i.e., whether from L1 into

L2 or the other way round. Below are the main constraints.

1.2.2.1.   Linguistic   Constraints: They   subsume:
1.2.2.1.1.Syntactic Constraints.

The different word order in SL and TL puts a heavy burden on the interpreter. A case in point is when interpreting a verbal sentence from Arabic into English. The verb may introduce a long nominal phrase. The interpreter has to store the verb and wait for the whole subject before he could retrieve and start the English rendition. Deprived of the sufficient time for manipulation, structural asymmetry often obliges the interpreter to commit pauses and delays among other things.

1.2.2.1.2. Semantic Constraints

These constraints compel the interpreter to exert a far more laborious effort than those originated by syntactic constraints, for as Jackendoff (1991: 96)puts it, "once one understands the meaning, the syntax follows naturally and automatically." Lexical incompatibility between SL and TL gives rise to slips, hesitations and even pauses, due to the interpreter's struggle with a difficult jargon term, a neologism or a blended word as in interpreting words like Macdonalization or the 1980s Reagonomics.

تطبيق أسلوب شركة ماكدونالد أو الاقتصاديات الريغانية.

To mitigate semantic constraints, the interpreter should be fully familiar with the speaker's topic and/or register.

1.2.2.1.3. Phonological and Prosodic Constraints

They include features that are non-existent in either SL or TL pertaining to segmental phonemes (vowels, consonants, consonant clusters, and diphthongs), suprasegmentals and prosodic features such as stress, intonation, pitch, rhythm and tempo. Many scholars rightly maintain that translating/interpreting is an intercultural communication act that requires bicultural competence .

1.2.2.1.4. Cultural and Phatic Constraints to cope with culture specificities whether religious, political or social such zakat, *intifada*, *autocracy* and *disco* in addition to institutional nomenclature exemplified in the different compounds with the Arabic *dar* (house) as in guest-house.دار الضيافة rest house, *dar al-istiraha* دار الإستراحة, orphanage *dar al- aytaam* دار الأيتام,radio/ broadcasting station *dar al-idaa'a* دار الإذاعة, The hereafter *dar al-baqa'* دار البقاء.

Other examples of culture specificities are the modes of address such as Mr. Miss. Mrs. Lord, أبو Abu or أم Umm plus proper noun as in Abu Ahmed أبو أحمد, Umm Ahmed or honorary titles such as معالي *ma'ali*, فخامة *fakhamat*, and phatic expressions of courtsey and salutaion such as the opening and closing greeting:

As-salam alaikum wa rahmutul-lahi wa barakatuhu :

السلام عليكم ورحمة الله وبركاته

whose natural equivalent in English could be no more than 'good morning / evening' or 'thank you'.

1.2.2.1.5. Paralinguistic and Psychological Constraints

These constraints include the speaker's tone and loudness of voice, the tempo of delivery and gestures as well as the psychological state of the interpreter and/or speaker as regards nervousness instead of self – composure. The laborious task of simultaneous decoding and encoding and his/her concern over accuracy of rendition puts him/her in a very stressful situation. The act of interpreting is inversely proportional to the above constraints and to such psychological factors as fatigue, timidity or stage fright for interpreters who have to directly address the audience. The constraints often trigger omissions, hesitations and even time lag.

1.2.2.3. Time Lag

Time lag refers to the time between the interpreter's reception of the speaker's utterance and his/her production. It is ear-tongue or hearing-voicing span. Time lag varies according to the nature of the SL message and the number, type and intensity of the aforesaid constraints. For example, the syntactic and lexical complexities and the pile-up of information segments may oblige the interpreter to lag behind the speaker to get a clear understanding, or at least the gist, of the message so as to reformulate it in the TL. Such lag puts a heavy burden on the short-term memory of the interpreter who might inevitably miss the subsequent segments of information and produce poorly cohesive structures and/or rushed sentences.

1.2.2.4.Interpreting Strategies : Discussed in Chapter Four below.

1.2.2.5.Quality Assessment and Audience Reception

Only bilingual readers, listeners or critics can accomplish translating/interpreting quality assessment. To be objective, the assessment has to be based on certain criteria, the most obvious of which is the semantic/stylistic fidelity to the original text/message. Fidelity entails such parameters as accuracy, grammaticality, acceptability, idiomaticity, and naturalness among others. Interpreting, however, requires other non – linguistic criteria for assessment.

On the other hand, monolingual audience who justify the act of translating/interpreting judge it in terms of other parameters, none of which pertains to fidelity which explicitly necessitates full knowledge of the two languages involved. The monolingual TL receptors, i.e., readers, judge translation in terms of their own language: style, grammar and TT intelligibility. The oral message receptors, i.e., listeners judge the interpreting act according to not only the above mentioned, but to non–linguistic criteria, at the top of which comes the message comprehensibility, which cannot be gauged in either-or terms, but graded along a spectrum ranging from fully comprehensible when the interpretation is clear and easy to understand to partially comprehensible and to totally incomprehensible. Besides, the audience rate the interpreting quality according to other criteria pertaining to smooth and fluent delivery, immediateness, pleasant voice, natural intonation and articulation, speech rate (whether fast or slow), self–composure, and idiolectal features such as the use of exaggerated fillers like *emmm, errr...*

Chapter Two

Translation Theories: A Historical Perspective

2.0. For almost two thousand years, translation theory has been concerned merely with outstanding works of art. The science of translation or 'translatology' has not emerge until the 1940s in an attempt to establish itself as a new discipline involving radical changes in the approach and classification, away from the age-old dichotomy of 'word vs. sense' or 'literal vs. free' translation, which has dominated the traditional translation theory since Cicero (cf. Snell-Hornby (1988: 1) . In point of fact, history of translation theory deals with the following kinds of questions explicitly stated by Baker:

> What translators have had to say about their art / craft / science; how translations have been evaluated at different periods; what kinds of recommendations translators have made, or how translation has been taught; and how this discourse is related to other discourses of the same period.
>
> (Baker, 2005:101)

More specifically, George Steiner in *After Babel* (1975:346-40) divides the literature on the theory, practice and history of translation into four periods which extend from Cicero to the present, albeit their overlap and loosely chronological structure.

2.1.The First Period

This period starts with the Romans. Eric Jacobsen (in Bassnett, 1988:48) goes so far as to hyperbolically propound that translation is a Roman invention though translation is as old as language itself. Translated documents were discovered in the third and the second millennium B.C., in ancient Egypt and in Iraq. It extends from the statements of Cicero and Horace on translation up to publication of Alexander Fraser Tytler's *Essay on the Principles of Translation* in 1791. It is perhaps the longest period as it covers a span of some 1700 years. The main characteristic of this period is that of 'immediate empirical focus', i.e., the statements and theories from the practical work of translating. Both Horace and Cicero, in their remarks on translation, make an important distinction between *word for word* translation and *sense for sense* translation. The underlying principle of enriching the native language and literature through translation leads to stress the aesthetic criteria of the TL product rather than the more rigid notions of 'fidelity'. Horace in his *Art of Poetry*, warns against overcautious imitation of the source model and slavish litertalism :

"A theme that is familiar can be made your own property so long as you do not waste your time on a hackneyed treatment; nor should you try to render your original word for word like a lavish translator, or in imitating another writer plunge yourself into difficulties from the which shame, or rules, you have laid down for yourself, prevent you from extricating yourself."

(Bassnett, 1988: 49

This period concludes by Tytler's definition of good translation as:

That in which the merit of the " original work is so completely transfused into another language, as to be as distinctly apprehended, and as strongly felt, by a native of the country to which that language belongs, as it is by those who speak the language of the original work". (in Bell,1991:

(11

From the above definition, Tytler introduces three 'laws':

1.The translation should give a complete transcript of the ideas of the original work.

2. The style and manner of writing should be of the same character with that of original.

3. The translation should have all the ease of original composition. (Ibid)

2.2. The Second Period:

This period, according to Steiner, runs up to the forties of the twentieth century. It is characterized as a period of theory and hermeneutic inquiry with the development of a vocabulary and methodology of approaching translation. 'Hermeneutics' is an interpretive approach developed by German Romantics, and named after the Greek word *hermeneuein*, meaning 'to understand'. One of the early theorists in this period is the French humanist Etienne Dolet who had propunded in 1540 a short outline of translation principles, entitled *'La maniere de bien traduire d'une langue en aultre* (How to Translate Well from One Language into Another) and established five principles for the translator (in Bassnett : 58) .

1. The translator must fully understand the sense and meaning of the original author, although he is at liberty to clarify obscurities.

2. The translator should have a perfect knowledge of both SL and TL.

3. The translator should avoid word-for-word renderings.

4. The translator should use forms of speech in common use.

5. The translator should choose and order words appropriately to produce the correct tone.

Dolet's principles , ranked as they are in a precise order, stress the importance of *understanding* the SL text as a primary requisite. His views were reiterated by George Chapman (559-1634), the great translator of Homer. In his dedication to the *Seven Books* (1598) Chapman asserts that "The work of a skilful and worthy translator is to observe the sentences, figures and forms of speech proposed in his author." He repeats his theory more fully in the *Epistle to the Reader* of his translation of *The Iliad*, (in ibid:59) stating that a translator must:

1. avoid word for word renderings;

2. attempt to reach the 'spirit' of the original;

3.avoid overloose translations, by basing the translation on a sound scholarly investigation of other versions and glosses.

John Dryden (1631-1700), in his *Preface to Ovid's Epistle* (1680), tackled the problems of translation by formulating three basic types (in Bassnett: 64):

1.**metaphrase,** or turning an author word by word, and line by line, from one language into another;

2. **paraphrase**, or translation with latitude, the Ciceronian 'sense-for-sense' view of translation;

3.**imitation**, where the translator can abandon the text of the original as he sees fit. Dryden claims to have steered "betwixt the two extremes of paraphrase and literal translation" which he likens to a person dancing on ropes with fettered legs(Ibid).

23

2.3. The Third Period:

This period, which is the shortest as it extends to less than three decades, starts with the publication of the first papers on machine translation in the 1940s, and is characterized by the introduction of structural and applied linguistics, contrastive studies in morphology and syntax among others which help the translator identify similarities and differences between NL and FL, and communication theory into the study of translation. It comprises two eras: first the pioneering era (1949-1954); the second the invention of the first generation of machine translation.

2.4. The Fourth Period:

The last period coexists with the third period as it has its origin in the early 1960s, and is characterized by a recourse to hermeneutic inquiries into translation and interpretation, i.e., by a revision of translation that sets the discipline in a wide frame which includes a number of other disciplines.

This contemporary period has witnessed the emergence of many new theories such as the ' polysystem theory, which has first arisen from the work of a group Russian literary theorists. The concept of the 'polysystem' has received considerable attention in the work of certain groups of translation scholars since the mid-1970s. The theory offers a general model for understanding, analyzing and describing the functions and evolution of literary systems, its specific application to the study of translated literature. These systems, whether in the original or translated texts subsume several levels: linguistic, cultural, and social, all of which overlap and interact with each other.

'Skopos theory' is another theory which was developed in Germany in the late 1970s (Vermeer, 1978). It reflects a shift from predominantly linguistic and rather formal theories to a more functionally and socio-culturally oriented concept of translation. The word '*skopos*' is derived form Greek as a technical term for the purpose of translation, i.e., skopos which must be defined before translation begins. The theory endeavours to meet the growing need in the latter half of the twentieth century for the translation of non-literary texts: scientific, academic papers, instructions for use, tourist guides, contracts, etc. According to this theory, the contextual factors surrounding the translation should not be ignored. These factors include the culture of the intended readers of the target text and the client who commissioned it, and more significantly the *function* which the text aspires to perform in that culture for those readers. Likewise, *pragmatics* stresses the principle of intentionality in translation, i.e. significance of the text or the author's intention, and that the 'comprehension of the intent', according to Nida, is a vital requisite of translation.

2.5. Translation Computerization Era

The invention of computer has led to aspire after an automatic machine translation (MT) wherein the computer is provided with the ST to be reproduced automatically or with the assistance of man as a semantically equivalent and well-formed text in the TL.

Translation-oriented computerized technology in general and machine translation (MT) in particular can be described as a complex and diverse field in which a wide range of 'actors', such as translation theorists, linguists, engineers among other researchers play a vital role in addition to evaluators of end-user groups including professional translators, trainers and translation companies.

MT is simply a translation performed either purely automatically by a computer or with human assistance which involves the preparation of the ST, i.e., pre-editing and/or product editing, i.e., post-editing. Historically, MT has undergone five periods of development (As-Safi, 2004:207-227), starting with the pioneering era followed by the second period which witnessed at mid-fifties the appearance of the first generation whose systems rely upon 'direct translation' wherein the ST words are replaced with TT words after conducting the required morpho-syntatic changes based on the contrastive differences between the SL and TL. The third period is initially characterized by stagnation of research but later by the development of the indirect approach of MT. The fourth period witnessed the appearance of the second generation, which is the product of 'rule-based approaches' based on the notion of translation as a process involving the analysis and representation of the ST meaning by TL equivalents. Furthermore, in this period there emerged other rule-based approaches which, according to Palumbo (00973-74) rely on rules that convert the abstract SL representation into an abstract TL representation. These systems require various transfer models for different language pairs.

The fifth period is marked with the third generation as the product of 'corpus-based approaches' which seem to have gained popularity in the early 1990s. It employs a reference corpus of TTs and STs, particularly statistical-based approaches which use algorithms to match the new TL segments with the built-in SL segments and their equivalents contained in the corpus, then compute the possibility that corpus-based TL equivalents are valid TL segments for the new text to be translated. (Quah, 2006: 196)

2.6. Arabs' Theorization

The Arabs, according to Baker (2005: 318), are credited with initiating the first organized, large-scale translation activity in history. This activity started during the reign of the Umayads (661-750) and reached its zenith under the Abbasids (750-1258), particularly during the reign of Al-M'mun (813-33) , known as the Golden Era of translation. Al-Ma'mun had founded in 830 the most important institute of higher learning in Islam, which also became the most celebrated center of translation in Arab history. *Bait Al-Hikma* (House of Wisdom), in Baghdad, functioned as an academy, library and translation bureau which had a personnel of 65 translators.

Two methods of translation had been adopted: the first, associated with Yuhana Ibn Al-Batriq and Ibn Na'ima Al-Himsi, was highly literal and consisted of translating each Greek word with an equivalent Arabic word, but when there is no equivalent, the Greek word is adopted. This method, as in all literal translations, was not successful so that many of their translations were later revised by Hunayn Ibn Ishaq with whom the second method was associated, which exercised translating sense-for-sense.

Thus it creates fluent translated texts which convey the meaning of the original without distorting the TL. Ibn Ishaq and his followers had apparently given priority to the requirements of the target language and readers, stressing the significance of readability and accessibility, and employing, what he called 'pleasant and limpid style which can be understood by the non-expert.'(Ibid: 321). A proponent theorist and one of the best-known writers in his time , albeit never been a practitioner, is Al-Jahiz (d.869) who sharply remarks in his statements about translators and translation, insisting that the translator can never do the original writer justice or express him with fidelity.

2.7. Contemporary Status of Translation Theory

It seems that there is no unanimity on the role played by theory in translation practice. Peter Emery (2000:105) cites Klein-Braley (1996:26) among others who maintain that 'theory' has no place in most university translation programmes and go so far as to declare that it should be discarded in favour of more practical work. But this scientifically and empirically unfounded view is easily refuted by the general consensus that any translation programme direly needs some sort of principled theoretical background, let alone a rigorous theory, to guide practice. We strongly concur with Bahumaid (1996:99) who characterizes the lack of theoretical component as a serious drawback in most Arab university translation programmes.

[Prof. A. B. As-Safi]

Chapter Three

Translation Theories:
A General Survey

3.0. According to Newmark (1981: 19), translation theory is concerned mainly with determining appropriate translation methods for the widest possible range of texts or text-categories. It also provides a frame work of principles, restricted rules and hints for translating texts and criticizing translations, a background for problem solving. Any theory should also be concerned with translation strategies adopted to address difficulties and problems in certain complicated texts. Likewise, Graham (in Ross,1981: 23-24 and 26) asserts that any substantial theory of translation assumes some formal inquiry concerning the general principles of accomplishment, the very principles which define an object and specify a method of study. A rigorous theory of translation would also include something like a practical evaluation procedure with specific criteria. A good survey of the theories of translation is perhaps best furnished by E. Nida (1976:66-79) who avers that due to the fact that translation is an activity involving language there is a sense in which any and all theories of translation are linguistic (ibid:66). He classifies these theories into three: philological theories, linguistic theories and socio-linguistic theories, the sequel of three diverse perspectives and different approaches to principles and procedures of translation. If the emphasis is on the literary texts, the underlying theories of translation are best deemed philological; if it is on structural differences between SL and TL, the theories may be considered linguistic; and finally if it is on a part of communication process, the theories are best described as sociolinguistic. However, a more comprehensive survey subsumes far more than Nida's three sets of theories as elaborated below.

3.1. Philological Theories

Philological theories rely upon 'philology' as the study of the development of language, and the classical literary studies. They are mainly concerned with the comparison of structures in the native and foreign languages, especially the functional correspondence and the literary genres in addition to stylistics and rhetoric. Nida explicitly states:

> The philological theories of translation are, of course, based on a philological approach to literary analysis. They simply go one step further; in place of treating the form in which the text was first composed, they deal with corresponding structures in the source and receptor languages

and attempt to evaluate their equivalences. Philological theories of translation are normally concerned with all kinds of stylistic features and rhetorical devices.

(Nida, 1976: 67-68)

3.2. Philosophical Theories

The most prominent proponent of these theories is George Steiner, who claims that his book *After Babel* (1975) is the 'first systematic investigation of the theory and practice of translation since the eighteen century.' He primarily emphasizes the psychological and intellectual functioning of the mind of translator. He elucidates that meaning and understanding underlie the translation process, averring that a theory of translation is essentially a theory of semantic transfer from SL into TL. He defines his 'hermeneutic approach' as " the investigation of what it means to ' understand a piece of oral speech or written text, and the attempt to diagnose the process in terms of a general model of meaning" (Steiner,1975:249.

He introduces his model in what he calls 'Hermeneutic Motion' to describe the process of literary translation. He looks upon the act of translation in the context of human communication across barriers of language, culture, time and personality, thus subdividing this motion into four stages (or moves). The first move is termed *trust* or *faith*, which consists of the translator's assumption that the source text contains 'a sense to be extracted and retrieved into and via his own language, although this is generally an unconscious action. The second move is referred to as the '*aggression, penetration* or *decipherment,* in which the translator "invades, extracts and brings home" the meaning of the original. The third move is termed '*incorporation, embodiment* or *appropriative use*'. Translation can introduce new elements into the target linguistic and cultural system. The fourth and final stage or move is labeled '*compensation, restitution or fidelity*' The translator must work to restore in his language what he has failed to recover from the original text.

3.3. Linguistic Theories

Linguistic theories of translation, according to Nida (1976: 69) , are based on a comparison of the linguistic structures of the STs and TTs, rather than a comparison of literary genres and stylistic features of the philological theories. Their development is due to two factors: first, the application of the rapidly expanding linguistics, the scientific study of language, to several fields such as cognitive anthropology, semiotics, pragmatics, and teaching translation/interpreting skills; and second, the emergence of Machine Translation (MT) which has provided a significant motivation for basing translation procedures on linguistic analysis as well as for a rigorous description of SL and TL (Nida, 1976: 70).

These theories are perhaps best represented by proponent figures, such as Eugene Nida, Roger Bell and J.C. Catford who opens his well-known book '*A Linguistic Theory of Translation*' with the words: "Clearly, then, any theory of translation must draw upon a theory of language – a general linguistic theory" (165:1) This book has been translated into Arabic by As-Safi (1983). Accordingly, '*Linguistic Translation*' (or *Linguistic Approach*) is a product of these theories which view translation as simply a question of replacing the linguistic units of the ST (source text) with "equivalent" TL units without reference to factors such as context or connotation. Catford (1965:20) defines translation (in Chapter One above) as a mere replacement of textual material in SL by equivalent textual material in the TL . Explicitly, 'equivalence' which is elaborated in Chapter Five below is a milestone in the linguistic theories .

According to Nida and Taber (1969:134) it is only a linguistic translation that can be considered 'faithful', because it "is one which only contains elements which can be directly derived from the ST wording, avoiding any kind of explanatory interpolation or cultural adjustment which can be justified on this basis." Nida (1976:75) suggests a three-stage model of the translation process. In this model, ST surface elements (grammar, meaning, connotations) are *analyzed* as linguistic kernel structures that can be *transferred* to the TL and *restructured* to form TL surface elements. His linguistic approach basically bears similarity with Chomsky's theory of syntax and transformational generative grammar.

Pertinent to linguistic theories is Newmark's binary classification of translation into semantic and communicative, which somehow resembles Nida's formal and dynamic equivalence. "Communicative translation," Newmark (1981:39) states, "attempts to produce on its readers an effect as close as possible to that obtained on the original. Semantic translation attempts to render, as closely as the semantic and syntactic structures of the second language allow, the exact contextual meaning of the original. These two approaches can best be illustrated in the following figure (Newmark,1981: 39):

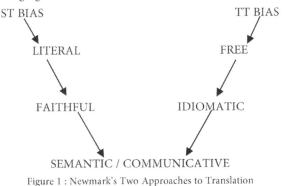

Figure 1 : Newmark's Two Approaches to Translation

The contribution of linguistics to translation is twofold: to apply the findings of linguistics to the practice of translation, and to have a linguistic theory of translation, as opposed to other theories such as the literary theory of translation. There are, however, differences among linguistic theories, the principal of which, Nida (Ibid) maintains, lies in the extent to which the focus is on surface structures or corresponding deep structures. Theories based on surface-structures comparisons involve the use of elaborate sets of rules for matching corresponding structures, whereas those based on deep-structures involve transformational analyses employed in teaching the methods of translation.

3.4. Functional Theories

The 1970s and 1980s witnessed a shift from the static linguistic typologies of translation and the emergence , in Germany, of a functionalist and communicative approach to the analysis of translation. These theories subsume the early work on text type and language function, the theory of translational action, skopos theory (Baker, 2005: 235-238; and Shuttleworth and Cowie, 2oo7:156-157) and text-analysis model.

3.4.1. Text-Type Theory

Built on the concept of equivalence, which is the milestone in linguistic theories, the text, rather than the word or sentence, is deemed the appropriate level at which communication is achieved and at which equivalence must be sought (Reiss , 1977: 113-14). Reiss links the functional characteristics of text types to translation methods. The main characteristics of each text type can be summarized as follows (pp.108-9):

3.4.1.1. Informative: It is concerned with 'plain communication of facts': information, knowledge, opinions, etc. The language dimension used to transmit the information is logical or referential; the content or 'topic' is the main focus of the communication.

3.4.1.2. Expressive: It denotes the 'creative composition' wherein the author uses the aesthetic dimension of the language.

2.4.1.3. Operative: The purpose is to induce behavioural responses, i.e., to appeal to or persuade the reader or 'receiver' of the text to act in a certain way.

3.4.1.4. Audiomedial: It refers to films and visual or spoken advertisements which supplement the other three functions with visual images, music, etc.

Reiss proposes (ibid, 20) 'specific translation methods according to text type'. These methods can be described as follows:

1. The TT of an informative text should transmit the full referential or conceptual content of the ST. The translation should be 'plain prose' without redundancy, but with the use of explication when required.

2. The TT of an expressive text should transmit the aesthetic and artistic form of the ST. The translation should use the 'identifying' method, with the translator adopting the stand point of ST author.

3. The TT of an operative text should produce the desired response in the TT receiver. The translation should create an equivalent effect among TT readers.

4. Audiomedial texts require the 'supplementary' method, written words with visual images and music. The text type approach moves translation theory beyond a consideration of lower linguistic levels, the

mere words beyond even the effect they create, towards a consideration of the communicative purpose of translation (Munday, 2001:76).

3.4.2. Translational Action Theory

This theory views translation as purpose-driven, product-oriented or outcome-oriented human interaction with special emphasis on the process of translation as message-transmission or a 'translational action from a source text, and as a communicative process involving a series of roles and players the most important of whom are the ST producer or the original author, the TT producer or the translator and the TT receiver, the final recipient of the TT. The theory stresses the production of the TT as functionally communicative for the reader, i.e., the form and the genre of the TT, for instance, must be guided by what is functionally suitable in the TT culture, which is determined by the translator who is the expert in the translational action and whose role is to make sure that the intercultural transfer takes place satisfactorily.

Nord (2007:18) elucidates that translating (i.e., translation process) is essentially a purposeful activity or behaviour as displayed in the following figure (Nord's,2007: 18 adapted) in which translation is viewed as a form of mediated intercultural communication:

Figure 2 . Translation as a form of Mediated Communication

3.4.3. Skopos Theory: As already mentioned in the fourth period of the historical survey in Chapter Two, skopos theory stresses the interactional, pragmatic aspects of translation, arguing that the shape of the TT should be determined by the function or 'skopos' (the Greek word for 'aim' or 'purpose') that it is intended to fulfill in the target context' , and it may vary according to the recipient. The corollary is that the translator should use the translation strategies which are most appropriate to achieve the purpose for which TT is intended, irrespective of whether they are deemed to be the 'standard' way to produce in a particular translation context; in short, when producing a TT, 'the end justifies the means.' It is worth noting that an awareness of the requirements of the skopos "expands the possibilities of translation, increases the range of possible translation strategies, and releases the translator from the corset of an enforced – and often meaningless – literalness (Vermeer,1989:42), It is the target readers who will prompt the translator to translate, to paraphrase or even re-edit the TT as the most appropriate strategy to be adopted in a given situation.

The skopos theory is criticized by the linguistically oriented approaches on the ground of the oversimplification that is inherent in functionalism, the focus on the message at the expense of richness of meaning and to the detriment of the authority of SL text (Newmark, 1991; in Baker, 2005:237). Another criticism of this theory is that even though a translation may indeed fulfill its intended skopos perfectly well, it may nevertheless be assessed as inadequate on other counts, particularly as far as lexical, syntactic, or stylistic decisions on the microlevel are concerned. (Baker, 237)

3.5 . Sociolinguistic Theories

These theories endeavour to link translation to communicative theory and information theory, with special emphasis on the receptor's role in the translation process. They do not completely overlook language structures, instead they deal with it at a higher level in accordance to their functions in the communicative process. These structures may involve rhetorical devices or figures of speech such as simile, metaphor, irony, hyperbole, etc., in both literary and non-literary texts. These theories require the translator exhibit language competence as well as language performance.

3.5.1. Interpretative Theory (or Theory of Sense)

This theory, originally designed to reflect the processes which are involved in *conference interpreting,* is associated with a group of scholars known as the Paris School . It is a reaction against some of the restricted views of linguistics of the time. The proponents of this theory argue that interpreters do not work merely with linguistic meaning, but also need to take into account such factors as the cognitive context of what has already been said, the setting in which the interpreting is taking place and the interpreter's own world knowledge (Lavault, 1996:97;

in Shuttleworth and Cowie:2007: 85). The corollary is that the focus should be on the intended meaning or the sense rather than the words of the ST.

3. 6. Systems Theories

3.6.1. Polysystem Theory

The polysystem theory, Baker (2005:176) maintains, proffers a general model for understanding, analysis and
describing the functioning and evolution of literary systems, but focuses particularly on specific application to the study of translated literature, which, according to Even-Zohar (2000:118, in Munday,2001:109) is a system in the way that:

1. the TL selects works for translation;

2. translation norms, behaviour and policies are influenced by other co-systems.

Polysystem theory also offers three insights into translation (Baker, 2005: 178):

1. It is more profitable to view translation as one specific instance of the more general phenomena of inter-systemic transfer. 2. Instead of limiting the discussion to the nature of the equivalence between ST and TT, the translation scholar is free to focus on the TT as an entity existing in the target polysystem. The approach to translation would accordingly be target-oriented, aiming at investigating the nature of the TT in terms of the features which distinguish it from other texts originating within a particular system. Furthermore, TTs cease to be viewed as isolated phenomena, but are rather thought of as

manifestations of general translation procedures which are currently prevalent in the target polysystem.

3. The TT is not simply the product of selections from sets of ready-made linguistic options, but is rather shaped by systemic constraints of a variety of types of language structure in addition to genre and literary taste.

3.6.2. Manipulation Theory

This theory is adopted by a group of scholars associated with a particular approach to the translation of literature, and to what is known as 'Manipulation School' and also as the 'Descriptive, Empirical or Systemic School (Hermans, 1995: -217 in Shuttleworth: 101-102).

According to this theory, translation implies a degree of manipulation of the ST for a certain purpose, because the translation process brings the TT into line with a particular model which should secure social acceptance in the target culture. "The approach to literary translation," Hermans (in Shuttleworth, ibid) asserts, "is descriptive, target-oriented, functional and systemic". Explicitly, the theory is in sharp contrast with linguistic theories because from the start it approaches translation not as science, but as an art which permits manipulation rather than equivalence, thus it is concerned with literary not technical translation. Accordingly, translation process is deemed a rewriting process and the translator is a re-writer who can alter or manipulate the ST in such a way as to be acceptable in the target language and culture.

3..6.3. Aesthetic Communication Theory

The above theory, we propound, is creativity-oriented specifically for literary translation, which is essentially an aesthetic communication between the translator and the target reader. It is also based on the nature of literature be it original or translated. It is perhaps conspicuously indisputable that literary translation, just like literary original composition, is not only informative, i.e., conveys lexical meanings, but also expressive or emotive. It performs a semantic and aesthetic binary function. In point of fact, information in literary texts is aesthetically framed, which distinguishes such texts from non-literary ones.

Literary composition, be it original or translated, is a dynamic texture of vivid stylistic variations; it has no room for monotony, dullness and stagnation. It caters to arouse the receptors' suspense, please them and/or invite their interest. To this end, it employs a foregrounded structure, highly elevated style and literary diction. (As-Safi, 2006:10).

Likewise, literary translation which should ideally be a work of literature is dynamic rather than static: it should be more like AN original rather than THE original work of art. Accordingly an aesthetically communicative, dynamic translation must:

1. Be dynamic rather than static (As-Safi, 1994) ;
2. Be creative and aesthetically informative/ communicative;
3. Comply with the target linguistic system;
4. Be appropriate, i.e., fit the context of the message;

5. Be natural and free from translationese (As-Safi,1996);
6. Be acceptable to the target audience or literary readership and;
7. Aspire to occupy a position in the target literature as any other original works of art.

Due to the above requirements, in addition to the intricate, hybrid and aesthetic nature of literary translation, one may well concur with Adams (1973: 92-101) in asserting that literary works are harder to translate than they were to compose, "for the original composition is the art of choosing the exactly right word or expression, and includes the option of changing and modification as deemed appropriate whereas the art of literary/ belletristic translation is the art of choosing among a set of possible compromises.

The following figure illustrates that translation is essentially a communicatively manipulated act.

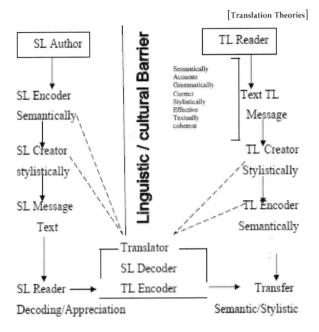

Figure 3: Translation as a Communicatively Manipulative Act.

The Above diagram demonstrates the multiple task of the translator as a decoder, appreciator, critic, encoder and creator who maintains an equilibrium to transfer the SL text semantically as well as stylistically. By necessity, he reads each word and each sentence in the ST as carefully as a critic before he transfers and finally composes it in the TL.

Such a transference and composition can never be achieved through literal, i.e., word-for-word translation which, Nida and Reybum (1981) rightly maintain, will inevitably tend to distort the meaning of the SL message or as Andre Lefevere (cited in Bassnett, 1996: 81) puts it, distorts the sense and the syntax of the original. Such a translation impedes the translator's work and stifles his creativity which is a manifestation of his competence and intelligence. It is, as Dryden (cited in Lefevere, 1992:102) puts it :

> Like dancing on ropes with
> fettered legs; a man may shun a fall
> by using caution, but gracefulness
> of motion is not to be expected:
> and when we have said the best of
> it, it's but a foolish task.

There is nothing new in repudiating literalism in translation, on which there is now almost a general consensus. Lefevere quotes Horace as antedating such an attitude:

> Word-for-word translation do not
> find mercy in our eyes, not because
> they are against the law of
> translation (as an act of
> communication) but simply
> because two languages are
> never identical in their vocabulary.
> Ideas are common to the

> understanding of all men but words
> and manners of speech are
> particular to different nations.
>
> (Bracketing is Lefevere's). (ibid)

3.7. Relevance Theory

Relevance theory is associated with pragmatics, which is primarily concerned with how language is used in communication, particularly with the way meaning is conveyed and manipulated by the participants in a communicative situation. In other words, pragmatics deals with 'speaker's meaning' and the way it is interpreted by the hearer(s), in what is known as 'implicature'. (Palumbo. 2009: 89) In translation, implicature can be seen as one level of equivalence between a ST and TT at which can be established. (The pragmatic equivalence is Baker's seventh kind, discussed in Chapter Five below). The theory, according to Gutt, is developed by Sperder and Wilson who emphasize the 'interpretive use ' of language' as distinct from the ' descriptive use. The former use is explicated by Gutt (2000:210) as follows:

> The fundamental characteristic of
> the interpretive use of language is
> not just the fact that two
> utterances interpretively resemble
> one another, but that one of them
> is intended to be relevant in virtue
> of its resemblance with the other
> utterance. In general terms, in

'reported speech' interpretively
used utterances "achieve relevance
by informing the hearer of the fact
that so-and-so has said something
or thinks something."

(The quotation is Sperder and Wilson's)

Baker (2005:182) points out that Gutt tries to describe
translation in terms of a general theory of human
communication based on the premise that the ability of human
beings to infer what is meant may be accounted for in terms of
observing the principle of relevance defined as achieving
maximum benefit at minimum processing cost. In other words,
relevance theory endeavours to give an explicit account of how
the information-processing faculties of the mind enable us to
communicate with one another. Its domain is therefore mental
faculties rather than texts or processes of text production (Gutt:
21). The theory then represents a shift from description to
explanation, as elucidated below.

Relevance theory is not a descriptive-classificatory approach. It
does not try to give an orderly description of complex
phenomena by grouping them into classes, but tries instead to
understand the complexities of communication in terms of
cause-effect relationship (Gutt, 2000: 21-22).

3.8. Towards a Comprehensive, Applicable Theory of Translation

It is perhaps a very arduous task to formulate a comprehensive, applicable theory amidst multiplicity, miscellany and disparity of the existing theories. Nevertheless, We try tentatively to furnish such a theory, depending particularly on some authentic references. First comes Webster's definition of 'theory' as a 'body of generalizations and principles in association with practice in a field of activity.' Manifestly, translation is intrinsically a practical activity from which generalizations can be inferred, and is in a dire need for principles to guide the practice. Generalizations are only inferences drawn from paradigms, instances of facts provided by contrastive analyses of various levels in both ST and TT: morphological, syntactic, textual and stylistic/rhetorical. When generalizations are universally applicable and predictable they become principles, norms, rules or laws to govern the translation activity.

In the same vein, Graham (1981: 24-26) asserts that any substantial theory of translation assumes some formal inquiry concerning the general principles which define an object and specify a method of study. Furthermore, a rigorous theory of translation would also include a practical evaluation procedure.

According to Reiss and Vermeer (in Shuttleworth, 2007:185) any theory, including one on translation, should contain: "(1) the statement of its basis, (2) the description of its object, and (3) an inventory of rules".

Likewise, Newmark (1981: 19) contends that translation theory's main concern is to determine "appropriate translation methods" and to provide " a framework of principles, restricted rules and hints for translating texts and criticizing translations." On the same lines, Longman Dictionary of Teaching & Applied Linguistics (p.691) defines 'theory' as " a statement of a general principle, based upon reasoned argument and supported by evidence, that is intended to explain a particular fact, event, or phenomena." Bell (1991: 24-25) also explicitly states: " A theory is an explanation of a phenomena, the perception of system and order in something observed. From the observation, data is collected to explain the theory which, according to Bell (1991:24), will lead to a model, as illustrated in the following figure:

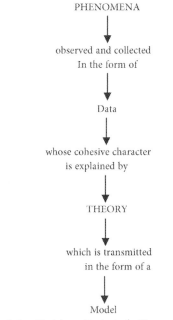

Figure 4: Bell's Translation Model as a Product of a Theory

Another example of a model is furnished by Nida (in Bassnett: 23) for the translation process:

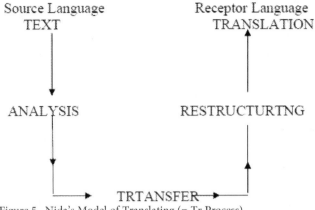

Figure 5 . Nida's Model of Translating (= Tr Process)

Ideally, Bell (p. 27) rightly maintains, a theory must reflect four characteristics:
1. empiricism : it must be testable;
2. determinism : it must be able to predict;
3. parsimony : it must be simple and economic;
4. generality : it must be comprehensive.

"A full, inclusive theory of translation," Holms (in Ibid) maintains, "must accommodate many elements which can serve to explain and predict all phenomena falling within the domain of translating (i.e., the process) and translation (i.e., the product), to the exclusion of all phenomena falling outside it". (Bracketing is mine). But instead of one theory which caters for both process and product, Bell (p. 26) envisages three types of theories of translation:

1.A theory of translation as **process** (i.e., a theory of translating): This would require a study of information processing and, within that, such topics as (a) perception, (b) memory and (c) the encoding and decoding of messages, and would draw heavily on psychology and psycholinguistics.

2. A theory of translation as a **product** (i.e., a theory of translated texts): This would require a study of texts not merely by means of the traditional levels of linguistic analysis (syntax and semantics) but also making use of stylistics and recent advances in text-linguistics and discourse analysis.

3. A theory of translation as both **process** and **product** (i.e., a theory of translating and translation): This would require the integrated study of both, and such a general theory is, presumably, the long-term goal for translation studies.

To the third type, i.e., process and product, we add an essential intermediary element between the process and the product, i.e., transfer. Accordingly, translation is a tri-phase activity. In fact, the intricate nature of translation makes it mandatory to relate the product to the tri-phase process (As-Safi, 1996), though the constituent phases are not autonomously separate from each other.

First comes the phase of decoding, whereby the original text is analysed for a thorough acquaintance both thematically and stylistically, that is, for full comprehension and stylistic appreciation. Here the translator performs the triple task of a reader, a critic and an interpreter: he has not only to comprehend the semantic units of the original text but also to be aware of the author's style and salient syntactic / rhetorical features when dealing with literary / belletristic text. The initial step in the textual analysis carried out conventionally and perhaps subconsciously by most translators is to segment the text into a number of units: words, phrases, clauses and sentences within each of which the distribution of denotative and connotative meanings are scanned. A pertinent test of intelligibility is purported by Nida (1964: 140). In his "cloze-technique" the reader is provided with a text in which, for example, every fifth word is deleted, and he is asked to fill in with whatever words that seem to fit the context best. The degree of comprehensibility is related to the degree of predictability. It is assumed that the easier it is for the reader to guess the next word in a sentence, the easier to comprehend the word in the given context and the greater the number of correct guesses, the greater the predictability and consequently the easier the text.

The second phase is that of "transcoding" or transfer. After acquainting himself with the original text, the translator usually starts to ascertain and record the equivalence in the target language for each of the elements he has already identified. In most cases, however, equivalence is far from being identical, or as Catford (1965: 27) puts it, "nearly always approximate, since every language is ultimately *sui generis*". Items are said to be equivalent in the two languages when they are interchangeable in a given situation. Lexically, equivalence appears to rest on the principle of bilingual synonymy: the notion that words are mere labels of real things goes back as far as Plato and carries over to some extent into De Saussure's concept of the sign (De Beaugrande, 1978: 98). In such a simplified view, translation consists of exchanging labels, consulting if need be a dictionary or an informant, and it underlies the awkward, literal or word-for-word transfer and what Dryden terms 'metaphrase'. Such a view has been recently questioned, by many linguists and celebrated translators, for true synonymy - the property of words to be mutually interchangeable in two contexts – is quite rare for most 'abstract' items, let alone the highly emotive or connotative, the language-specific and culture-specific ones.

In consequence, the translator cannot easily or immediately furnish solutions to all problems regarding equivalence albeit resorting to an exhaustive search through all available reference materials. If an equivalent expression cannot be located, he must find some parallel expression that will yield approximately the same kind of effect produced by the original. Idioms, and figures of speech, such as allegory, metaphor, parable or simile, are cases in point. The metaphor baidha' (white) in the Arabic expression *lailatun baidha'* ليلة بيضاء cannot be rendered as such (i.e. white night) but sleepless night; similarly, the word 'teeth' becomes 'arm' in Arabic in the following idiomatic utterance: 'He would have given his back teeth for such a chance:

" مستعد للتضحية حتى بذراعه في سبيل ذلك".

And the English simile: "as cool as cucumber" might produce a rather ridiculous effect in Arabic when rendered literally instead of رابط الجـأش meaning: calm at time of danger. Yet even when the task of harmonizing grammatically correct structures is accomplished, the product of transfer may be accurate but perhaps wooden: it is something more than a gloss and something less than a literary work.

The third and final phase is recoding the transferred message in the target language, complying with its linguistic as well as literary conventions of the literary texts so as to be as semantically accurate and aesthetically effective as the original. A translation of a literary work of art can justify itself only when it comes to be a literary work, occupying an appropriate position in the target literature comparable to the status of the original in the source literature and at the same time resembling the original in every respect. And as Adams (1973: 100) puts it, "a proper literary translation does not simply convey to us the elements of the original in such fullness as may be, but conveys them to us in something of the same order and structure of relatedness as the original". If the product sounds mediocre, in other words, if it reads as THE original and not AN original, the translator has not gone far enough in fulfilling his function, that is, his product is lacking in aesthetic values, as it has failed to transmit the literariness and felicity of the original. The ideas may have been accurately reproduced but aesthetically wanting.

On the other hand, he will have gone too far should his translation depart too radically from the semantic content and/or literary values of the original. This very delicate yet difficult equilibrium intensifies the plight of the literary translator, for his 'recreation' of the original should not render translation as a mere imitation or an artistically embellished 'edition'. Besides his literary or rhetorical competence, he has to be very tactful and eclectic in his approach. For instance, of the three methods of translation which Dryden distinguishes in his preface to the translation of *Ovid's Epistles* (1680), 'metaphrase' or word-for-word might shackle the translator to the original work whereas 'paraphrase' or sense-for-sense and 'imitation', whereby he abandons the text of the original, both bestow upon him a freedom which would necessarily distance him from the original. Therefore, one may well concur with Adams (1973: 11), who asserts that literary works are harder to translate than they were to compose, "for the original composition is the art of choosing the exactly right word or expression, and includes the option of changing and modification as deemed appropriate, whereas the art of translation is the art of choosing among a set of possible compromises; it simply does not allow that important option".

Chapter Four

Translation and Interpreting Strategies

4.0. A translation strategy is a procedure for solving a problem encountered in translating a text or a segment of it (Baker, 2005:188). Given the distinction between micro-level and macro-level problems, strategies can be divided between **local** ones which deal with text segments and **global** strategies which deal with the whole texts . Both local and global strategies interact with relevant elements of the translator's background knowledge : critical awareness of the style and content of similar texts, of linguistic conventions, register and intuitions about what constitutes the target language (ibid).

Translation strategies can be categorized into **general** and **specific** strategies.

4.1. General strategies: they deal with different text- types

4.2. Specific strategies: they tackle a certain text- type, readership and skopos, i.e. the function or purpose of translation. These strategies are of four sub-categories

4.2.1. Domestication strategy, also called normalization or naturalization strategy, is employed to bridge cultural gaps and achieve intelligibility in line with the hermeneutic approach which focuses on interpretation and grants the translator the right to manipulate the text so as to make it natural, comprehensible and readable (for naturalness in translation, see As-Safi, 1997) , an approach in which the original text undergoes adaptation so as to be re-created to comply with the target linguistic and cultural conventions and to fulfill the function or purpose of translation, i.e. skopos.

This strategy is often adopted by literary translators as seen in the translations of the following excerpts from Shakespeare's *The Merchant of Venice* into Arabic by Khalil Mutran, 'Amer Al-Buhairi, Hussein Amin and Mohammed Al-Anai. They have all replaced the currency of the time 'ducat', which is not readily understandable by the Arab audience by a contemporary 'dinar', and even changed the number 'fourscore' into 'seventy'.

Tubal (Addressing Shylock):
Your daughter spent in Genoa, as I heard one night, fourscore ducats. (111. 2. 90-95) **Anani:**

توبال (مخاطبا شايلوك):

سمعت أن جيسيكا قد أنفقت في ليلة واحدة سبعين دينارا. (عناني ,
122 ص) And in Launcelot's allegory of referring to the Greek mythology such as the sea monster or the great rock 'Scylla' and the swift sea swirl 'Charybdis' of which the Arab audience are ignorant:

Launcelot:
Truly, then, I fear you are damned both by father and mother, thus when I shun Scylla your father, I fall into

Charybdis your mother. Well, you are gone both ways. (111. 5. 13-15) **Buhairi**

وعندئذ أخشى حقا أن تكوني ملعونة من جهتي الأب والأم، فعندما هربت من أبيك شيل فقد أخطأت في حق امك شاريديس، فأنت هالكة من الجهتين (عامر محمد بحيري: ص 193-194)

◌ So does **Al-Wakeel**:

اني لأخشى عليك اذن أن تكوني ملعونة الأب والأم جميعاً فإذا طبتَّ لسفينتك النجاة من الارتطام بصخرة أبيك، لم يكتب لها النجاة من صخرة أمك وهكذا أنت هالكة لا محالة. (الوكيل, ص 102-103)

Mutran:

أخشى أن تكوني هالكة من جهة الاب ومن جهة الام معاً، فاذا أردت لك النجاة من ناحية الصخر: ابيك وقعت من ناحية الهوة: امك، فأنت بتمام الراحة..هالكة من هنا ومن هناك.

Amin goes so far in his domestication as to allude to a common Arabic proverb: كالمستجير من الرمضاء بالنار

فأنت اذن ملعونة من الجهتين : الاب والام، ان تجنبت الرمضاء (وهي ابوك) وقعت في النار (التي هي امك) وبهذا يكون مصيرك مظلما في الحالتين.

Obviously Amin is alluding to the Arabic poetic line:

المستجير بعمر عند كربته كالمستجير من الرمضاء بالنار

It corresponds to the English proverb:

> Out of the frying pan into the fire.

4.2.2. Compensation strategy.

Compensation is, according to Sandor Hervey and Ian Higgins (1992:248), the technique of making up for the translation loss of significant features of the ST approximating their effects in the TT through means other than those used in the ST, that is making up for ST effects achieved by one means through using another means in the TL. In translating most of the jurisprudential maxims, loss is apparently inevitable ; hence this strategy has been maximally utilized. This strategy can be categorized into four sub-strategies (ibid) to which we add a fifth one.

4.2.2.1. Compensation in kind

Compensating for a particular type of a textual effect deemed to be untranslatable into the TT by using a textual effect of a different type in the TT . An example for that is the Arabic emphatic devices such as the *Lam* and *Noon* as in *linabluwnnakum* (*Surely We will try you*), compensated by lexical items such as *truly ,verily, surely*.. etc., as in the Qur'anic *aya* 155 of *surat Al-Baqara* (*the Cow*).

4.2.2.2. Compensation in place

Compensating for the loss of a particular textual effect occurring at a given place in the ST, by creating a corresponding effect at a different place in the TT. An instance for this compensatory strategy is employed to make up for an inevitable loss such as figures of speech pertaining to schemes or tropes, as in compensating for the loss of alliteration by employing assonance or vice versa .

4.2.2.3. Compensation by merging

Condensing the features carried over a relatively longer stretch of the ST into a relatively shorter stretch of TT , as in translating the phrase [*jabara khatirahu*] into one single lexical item, the English verb *consoled* or *comforted* and the lexical item 'sacrifice' for three Arabic synonymous words

التضحية والفداء والعطاء

4.2.2.4. Compensation by splitting

Distributing the features carried in a relatively shorter stretch of the source text over a relatively longer stretch of the TT; as in translating the word(*ijtihad*اجتهـاد) which literally means *diligence*, but in a religio-legal context it is translated into a long stretch of words such as: "reasoned inference or individual or independent religious opinion or intellectual effort." Another example is the translation of the Islamic term (*al-Ihraam*الاحرام) into English as "a state in which one is prohibited to exercise certain deeds and practices that are religiously permitted at another state or circumstance."

4.2.2.5. Compensation by Addition

To compensate for the inevitable loss in the translation of *Du'a Al-Karawan* (The Call of the Curlew) with its poetic style and highly classical and Quranic language, we have painstakingly attempted to achieve some gains by adding, for instance, an idiom or a metaphor that has no counterpart in the original, as exemplified in 6.2. below.

4. 2.3. Strategy of Addition

In translating Launcelot's speech, 'Anani adds Hellfire to the original text:

63

الواقع أن جهنم مثواك ...من والدك ومن والدتك! فالمثل يقول: ان
ينجو الملاح... من صخرة (سيلا) .. والرمز لوالدك هنا – لن ينجو من
دوامة ذلك البحر ... عند (خرييبيديس) – والرمز لامك طبعا ! ولهذا
فهلاكك محتوم من ناحيتين . (عناني ص 152)

4.2.4. Strategy of Elaboration and Explication

In order to communicate the original message in an intact
manner to the recipient, the translator sometimes resorts to
elaboration or explication. Here is again an example from
Shakespeare's *The Merchant of Venice* :

Shylock:

What news on the Rialto ?

Word by word or literal translation into Arabic is:

ما أخبار ريالتو ؟

Such translation is clearly unintelligible , for the proper noun
could be understood as a name of a person rather than stock
market. Anani has replaced the proper noun by what it means in
Arabic:

ما أخبار البورصة ؟

By utilizing the strategy of addition, it can be rendered as

ما أخبار بورصة ريالتو ؟

4.2.5. Strategy of Approximation and Compromise :

This strategy endeavours to create an equilibrium or balance
between the SL aesthetic and cultural values which are acceptable
or unacceptable in the TL. We followed this strategy among
others, in translating Taha Hussein's *Du'a Al-Karawan* (the Call
of the Curlew) into English, as it is stated in the preface:

64

'The dilemma facing the present translator is how to bring about an equilibrium whereby the original aesthetic flavor is transferred into English without hindering genuine comprehension or producing something that can be rejected as totally "UN-English". In many cases, only an approximation, rather than complete translation, is possible in order to present a natural, acceptable rendition.'

(As-Safi,1980)

4.3. Interpreting Strategies

4.3.1. Compensation Strategy

Unlike the translator who enjoys the availability of time and resources, the interpreter is often obliged to have recourse to compensation strategies to ease the burden of constraints, to achieve a smooth performance and fluid ideas and to improve the pace of delivery.

4.3.2. Syntactic Modification Strategy

To eliminate or reduce delays and to counter the risk of lagging behind the SL speaker, the interpreter starts simultaneously uttering before he perceives the whole idea. This entails carrying out certain syntactic adjustments. For example, in interpreting from English into Arabic, the interpreter employs a nominal sentence(SVO), usually beginning with the particle <u>inna</u> إنَّ rather than the normally preferred verbal sentence in Arabic (VSO). By doing so, he could reduce the time required to wait until the speaker utters the verb that might follow a long noun phrase with sometimes embedded phrases and clauses, e.g.,

> On November 1, after a month of clashes, Faris's cousin, Shadi, a young man who had resentfully joined the Palestinian police <u>was killed</u> in a confrontation in Gaze. (International Herald Tribune, Tuesday, December 12, 2000).

> في الأول من نوفمبر (تشرين الثاني)
> وبعد شهر من المصادمات فإن ابن
> عم فارس، شادي وهو شاب التحق
> مؤخراً في الشرطة الفلسطينية قُتل في
> مواجهة في غزة.

Other examples can be cited in the anaphora/cataphora in English and Arabic and masculine gender of common nouns, e.g.,

> Coaches <u>are</u> indispensable for training sport teams. The new coach has a long experience with international teams in many European, Asian and African countries. <u>She</u> coaches the tennis team at the weekend.

> المدربون لا يستغني عنهم في
> تدريب الفرق الرياضية، **والمدرب**
> **الجديد** ذو خبرة طويلة مع فرق
> عالمية في عدة أقطار أوروبية

أسيوية وأفريقية، وإنها / وهي تدرب
فريق التنس في نهاية كل أسبوع.

4.3.3. Segmenting and Chunking Strategy

The interpreter resorts to this strategy when the SL speaker utters a lengthy sentence which has to be 'sliced' into sense units so as to cope with the short-term memory. Conversely, he may combine short sentences into compound or complex ones.

4.3.4. Lining up or Queuing Strategy

According to this strategy, the interpreter delays rendering a less significant information segment amidst a heavy load period of piled up information and then catches up in any lulls that occur later. (EI- Shiyab and Hussien, 2000; 556.) This strategy may assist the interpreter to reduce lag, but the delayed segment may not be cohesively compatible with the whole flow of delivery and thus may disrupt the thematic progression.

4.3.5. Calquing Strategy

To mitigate the effects of time constraints and to avert any anticipated lexical difficulty, the interpreter may imitate the SL lexical patterns and collocations and hence produce a literal, 'verbatim' rendition, e.g,

هذه الحادثة تختلف عن غيرها من الحوادث، فهي تتميز عما
سبقها من الحوادث في خطورة نتائجها.

Interpretation:

This incident is different from other incidents, for it is distinguished from previous ones in its gravity of consequences.

Translation:

This incident, unlike others, has unprecedented consequences.

4.2.6. Paraphrasing Strategy

Contrary to the above strategy, the interpreter may resort to paraphrase in encountering a SL culture-specificity, hence it may be rightly called " Exegetic Strategy", e.g., الطواف at-tawaaf going round AL-Ka'ba; running between Safa and Marwa during السعي as-sa'i, in pilgrimage, or demagnetize يزيل الخصائص المغناطيسية

4.3.7. Approximation Strategy

When the interpreter does not find a direct TL equivalent or fails to remember it, he can produce an alternative that has common semantic features, e.g,

opium poppy:الخشخاش) (drugs) instead of مخدرات

4.3.8. Borrowing Strategy

To cope with the speaker and maintain a rapid pace of delivery, the interpreter may have recourse to loan words through transliteration, e.g.,

video, stadium, cinema, UNESCO

4.3.9. Ellipsis Strategy

It is a strategy of reduction whereby some SL words are deleted when they are believed superfluous, repetitious or redundant, e.g.

(I) see you later سأراك فيما بعد

He is dead and you alive. أنه ميت وأنت حي ترزق.

[Prof. A. B. As-Safi]

Part Two

Basic Theoretical Issues

Chapter Five

Translation Equivalence

Equivalence is a key concept in the translation process in general and in the linguistic theories in particular. Ideally, equivalence is a bilingual synonymy or sameness based on lexical universals and cultural overlaps (As-Safi, 1996:11). Linking equivalence to substitution, Steiner (1998:460) believes that equivalence is sought by means of substitution of 'equal' verbal signs for those in the original. Baker (2005:77) rightly maintains that equivalence is a central concept in translation theory, albeit certain miner controversies about this concept. Proponents define equivalence as relationships between ST and TT that allows the TT to be considered as a translation of the ST in the first place.

Equivalence relationships are also believed to hold between parts of STs and parts of TTs. Many theorists think that translation is based on some kind of equivalence depending on the rank (word, sentence or text level). It must be acknowledged here that this equivalence in Arabic and English is in many cases unattainable on all levels.

5.1. Typologies of Equivalence

In surveying the typologies of equivalence, Baker (2005:77) cites on the word level **referential** or **denotative** equivalence between the SL and TL words which refer to the same thing in the real world, in addition to **connotative equivalence** where the SL and the TL words are expected to trigger the same or similar associations in the minds of the native speakers of the two languages. She bases typologies on Koller (1989:187-191) who presents what he calls **text-normative equivalence** in which the SL and TL words have the same effect on the SL and TL readers, which he also calls **pragmatic equivalence** (ibid). She refers to Nida's (1964) **dynamic equivalence** which aspires at creating similar response on the TL readers, so as to make translation communicative as contrary to **formal equivalence** which underlies literal translation. Based on Nida's classification of equivalence into formal vs. dynamic, As-Safi (1994) propounds two types of translation: static or literal and dynamic which is non-literal and even creative translation, especially in rendering literary texts (as elaborated in literary theories of translation above).

 Four types of translation equivalence are also distinguished by Popovic (in Bassnett, 1988: 32):

(1) **linguistic equivalence**: where there is homogeneity on the linguistic level in both the original and text;

(2) **paradigmatic equivalence**, where there is equivalence of the elements of a paradigmatic expressive axis, the elements of grammar, which Popovic sees as being a higher category than lexical equivalence;

(3) **stylistic equivalence,** where there is 'functional equivalence of elements in both original and translation

aiming at an expressive identity with an invariant of identical meaning; and

(4) textual (syntagmatic) equivalence, where there is equivalence of the syntagmatic structuring of a text; i.e. 'equivalence' of form and shape.

Pertinently, however, three things of great import are to be considered:

(1) equivalence is achieved when items in the original and translation have some common features in their contexts;

(2) the degree of contextual meaning is proportionate to the number of common features: equivalence increases as the number of common features increases; and

(3) translation may be ranged on a general scale of evaluation of accurate to inaccurate according to the degree of equivalence of the lexical items in both texts.

On the word level too, Hann (1992, in Baker, 2005:78) categorizes equivalence relationships into four, to which we may propound a fifth one.

One-to-one equivalence where there is a single expression in the TL for a single SL expression;

One-to-part-of-one equivalence wherein a TL expression covers part of the concept designated by a single SL expression as in the equivalence of the concept *zakat* into English as *alms or charity* which reveals part, but not the whole concept which denotes a regular , obligatory charity or more elaborately a certain fixed proportion of the wealth(2.5%) of every

Muslim to be paid yearly for the benefit of the needy in the Muslim community;

One-to-many equivalence wherein more than one TL expression for a single SL expression as in the English words *of kinship*, i.e. uncle which denotes paternal or maternal *uncle*, *spouse* for either husband or wife , *cousin* for the son or daughter of the uncle or aunt; in addition to the semantic level, this kind of equivalence can be seen on the syntactic level wherein, for example the Arabic diminutive nouns may have more than one lexical item, e.g. *nuhayr* نهير small river or rivulet.

Many-to-one wherein more than one TL lexical item for a single SL expression or lexical item, which reverses the above type.

Nil or zero equivalence wherein there is no TL expression for an SL expression, such as the word *ijtihat* **or**
mujtahid and *qiyas* and many other Islamic concepts which have no equivalence in English. This kind of non-equivalence has let to the phenomenon of borrowing among languages as it is found in many words in English and Arabic, such as **Television, Vedio** in Arabic and **Algebra** in English among many examples.

Before concluding equivalence, it is worth referring to Baker's *In Other Words* which is devoted in six chapters to six types of equivalence, namely:

1. Equivalence at word level which has just been discussed above;

2. Equivalence above the word level exemplified in collocation, idioms and fixed expressions;

3. Grammatical equivalence which deals with the diversity of grammatical categories across languages and word order;

4. Textual equivalence which deals with thematic and information structures;

5. Textual equivalence which focuses on cohesion externalized by substitution and ellipsis, and merging syntactic structures by conjunctions and finally;

6. Pragmatic equivalence which deals with coherence, implicature or the process of interpretation and translation strategies.

The common types of equivalence propounded by Baker that are pertinent to the process of transference between English and Arabic are pragmatic, lexical and grammatical, the last of which requires further elaboration. In Arabic, the nominal (verbless) sentences correspond to verbal sentences. For example, the following nominal sentences expressing jurisprudential maxims must be rendered into verbal counterparts in English:

الأمور بمقاصدها

Matters are judged by intentions.

الخراج بالضمان

Yield is guaranteed.

جناية العجماء جبار.

The beast's injury is squander.

العبرة في العقود للمقاصد والمعاني لا للالفاظ والمباني

In contracts, intentions and meanings, not words and
structures, shall be taken into consideration.

5.1.1. Collocational/Idiomatic Equivalence
5..1.1.1. Collocational Equivalence

Collocation refers to a sequence of co-occurring words or
simply as, Firth puts it, "the company words keep together", in a
combination in which a word tends to occur in relatively
predictable ways with other words, often with restrictions on the
manner of their co-occurrence, as explicitly seen in restricting
certain verbs or adjectives to certain nouns or certain
prepositions.

Collocational restrictions are described by Baker (1992: 285) as
'semantically arbitrary' because they do not logically follow from
the propositional meaning of the word outside the collocational
combination. It is the collocates, Larson (1984: 155) contends,
that determine which sense is indicated in a given phrase. Larson
(ibid) cites the example of the word 'dress' which has two
drastically different meanings in the phrase 'dress the chicken'
and 'dress the child'. To 'dress a chicken' involves 'taking the
feathers off' whereas 'dressing a child' is 'putting clothes on'.
Likewise, the adjective 'good' denotes two divergent meanings in
the phrases: 'good time' and 'good Friday'. As-Safi (1994: 69-70)
cites fifty different meanings of the adjective 'good' before fifty
nouns.

It is widely accepted that to produce an acceptable, accurate or appropriate TL equivalent for a SL counterpart poses a challenge even to the most competent and experienced translator. Achieving appropriate collocations in the TT, Hatim and Mason rightly assert, has always been seen as one of the major problems a translator faces, because SL interference may escape unnoticed, and by corollary, an unnatural collocation will flaw the TT . The translator's arduous task is due to the semantic arbitrariness of collocations as explicated by the following examples. We normally say in English "make a visit", but not "perform a visit". Baker (1992:47ff) points out that synonyms and quasi- or near-synonyms often have quite different sets of collocates: "break rules" but not "break regulations", or "wasting time" but not "squandering time, "strong tea" but not "powerful tea". Baker (ibid) also gives the example of the verb "drink" in English which collocates naturally with liquids like "juice and milk", but not with "soup". In Arabic, on the other hand, the verb "drink" collocates with almost all sorts of liquid, hence it collocates with "soup", e.g., yashrabu-l-hasaa"a يشرب الحساء .

All the above examples and others below display that collocations cannot be literally transferred from SL into TL. Consider the verb "catch" in the following collocations:

catch a fish	يصطاد سمكة
catch flue	يصاب بالانفلونزا
catch the train	يلحق بالقطار
catch the meaning	يفهم المعنى

79

catch attention	يستحوذ على الانتباه
catch one's breath	يلتقط أنفاسه (يستريح)

Dr. Reem Salah of Ptera University has asked her MA students to render 24 collocations of the adjective "executive" plus noun, as a test of translation competence:

An executive appearance

Executive bathroom

Executive corporate

Executive decider

Executive decision

Executive delay

Executive disease

Executive Friday

Executive house

Executive inn

Executive investor

Executive lunch

Executive manager

Executive Monday

Executive order

Executive parking

Executive project

Executive raincoat

Sale executive

Executive session

Executive summary

The company executive

Executive white trash

Executive workout

The above collocations obviously pose a difficult problem to a translator. There is another category of collocations that are almost literally rendered into Arabic which seems to have accommodated them as 'borrowed collocations. Here are some of them.

A black market	سوق سوداء
Adopt a plan/project	يتبنى خطة/مشروعا
Anarchy prevailed	سادت الفوضى
At a stone throw	على مرمى حجر
Blind confidence	ثقة عمياء
Blind imitation	تقليد اعمى
By sheer coincidence	محض مصادفة
Devote time	يكرس وقتا
Draw a policy	يرسم سياسة
Fire lines	خطوط النار
Exert an effort	يبذل جهدا
Hard currency	عملة صعبة
Honourable defeat	هزيمة مشرفة
Kill time	يقتل وقتا
On equal footing	على قدم المساواة
Point of view	وجهة نظر
Policy of rapproachement	سياسة التقريب
Political tension	توتر سياسي
Raise the level	يرفع المستوى
Safety valve	صمام امان
Save a situation	ينقذ موقفا
Starting point	نقطة البدء
Show interest	يبدي اهتماما
Striking force	قوة ضاربة
Teach sb a lesson	يلقن (شخصا) درسا

81

| Turning point | نقطة تحول |
| War of nerves | حرب أعصاب |

The following collocations assume the form of simile:

as+adj+as+ noun or like + noun

As brave as a lion	شجاع شجاعة الأسد
As cunning as a fox	ماكرمكر الثعلب
As fast as an arrow	سريع سرعة السهم
As innocent as a child	بريء براءة الطفل
As obstinate as a mule	عنيد عناد البغل
As slow as a tortoise	بطيء بطء السلحفاة
As strong as a lion	قوي قوة الأسد
As strong as a horse	قوي قوة الحصان
As strong as a an ox	قوي قوة الثور
As sweet as sugar/honey	حلو حلاوة السكر/الشهد
As clear as a day	واضح وضوح النهار
To talk like a child	يتحدث حديث الاطفال
To behave like children	يتصرف تصرف الأطفال
To run like the wind	يجري جري الرياح
To chatter like monkeys	يلغو لغو القردة

Chapter Six

Translation Loss and Gain

6.1. Translation Loss

Due to the discrepancies between English and Arabic as two languages of different families, one is Endo-European and the other Semitic, loss in translation is very common, varied and sometimes inevitable vis-à-vis avertable loss. Losses occur on all language levels: morphological, syntactic, textual and stylistic/rhetorical. It is , perhaps axiomatic to propound that the more meticulously and consummately the text texture is, the more inevitable losses are expected, as in the plethora of translations of the glorious Qur'an. Gain, on the other hand, is not only rare but also not always feasible. To bring about some gain in the translated text is a laborious task on the part of the competent translator who has to resort to certain strategies, such as those of compensation, domestication, annotation and explication. On the textual level, for instance, the translator may utilize exophoric reference; and on the stylistic/rhetorical level he/she may adopt the strategy of compensation whereby he could plant in the TT a metaphor equivalent to non-metaphor in the ST to atone for an inevitable loss of a preceding rhetorical feature in the ST.

Furthermore, an equilibrium should be maintained with regard to loss and gain in the translation which aspires after merit.

It is perhaps unanimously accepted that complete symmetry or sameness can hardly exist between languages descending from the same family, let alone those belonging to remote origins, which results in divergency on all planes. In fact, the more divergent the languages are, the more losses in translating from one language into another, English and Arabic are not an exception.

The asymmetrical character of these two languages underlies the linguistic/stylistic discrepancies on phonological, morphological, syntactic, semantic, textual, stylistic and cultural levels. Cultural differences, to take the last level, give rise to lexical gaps evinced in incongruous ideological, social and ecological terms which relate to highly sensitive issues such as religion and politics or those pertaining to institutions and nomenclature. Hence the process of translation between Arabic and English is sometimes clogged up by linguistic, rhetorical and cultural barriers which engender inevitable losses with very serious consequences especially in dealing with a highly sacred text like the Qur'an.

6.1.1. Kinds and Levels of Loss

There are two kinds of loss:

First, **inevitable loss**: It occurs because of the divergent systems of the two languages regardless of the skill and competence of the translator who cannot establish equivalence and therefore resorts to compensatory strategies. Second is an **avertable loss** which is attributed to translator's failure to find the appropriate equivalence. Both kinds of loss can be seen on all levels.

6.1.1.1. Morphological Level

On the morphological level, Arabic infix is an essential element in the morphological structure of the tri-literal root as in the infix *alaf* which indicates duality and reciprocality among other things, e.g., *faa'ala* فاعلor *tafaa'ala* تفاعل The infix in English, on the other hand, is restricted to few count nouns as in *tooth* (sing) and *teeth* (pl). To compensate for this loss, the translator opts to add a reciprocal pronoun, i. e., *each other* or *one another*, e. g.,

في الدائرة يتقابلان. أو يتقابلان في الدائرة -

- They meet each other/ one another in the office.

Likewise, the divergent number systems in the two languages engender grave loss unless skilfully compensated. Arabic classifies count nouns into three categories: singular, dual and plural; whereas English has a binary classification whereby count nouns are either singular or plural. To transfer duality from Arabic into English, a lexical item such as *both or two* must be added by way of compensation .

Unless compensated for, this loss may cause inaccurate intelligibility, ambiguity or misinterpretation, especially in dealing with a sacred text like the Qur'an. In *Al-Rahman* (Most Compassionate) *sura*, the *aya* فبـأي الآء ربكـما تكـذبان

repeated 31 times evinces duality in *rabbikumaa* ربكما (your Lord : Lord of the two of you) and *tukadhibaan* تكذبان (you *both* deny) where the English pronouns denote either singular or plural.

According to the majority of classical commentators and exegists, the dual form of address is meant to refer to two invisible beings, i.e.,*jinn* and mankind (see Az-Zamkhashari, bn Kathir, Qarani, among others). Al-Razi, however, maintains the duality of address, but he thinks the reference is the two categories of human beings, i. e., men and woman, to both of whom the Qur'an is addressed. In fact the whole *sura* is a symphony of duality which leads to Unity: all creation is in pairs (see footnote 5180 in the translation referred to as 'Mushaf Al-Madinah An-Nabawiyah published by King Fahd Holy Qur'an Printing Complex). In this *sura*, the things and concepts are presented in pairs: sun and moon, stars and trees, corn and plants, two easts and two wests, pearl and coral, Majesty and Honour, jinn and mankind (repeated 4 times), fire and brass, forelocks and feet, rubies and coral , date palms and pomegranates, green cushions and beautiful mattresses, equivalent in Arabic to:

الشمس والقمر - النجم والشجر - الحبّ والريحان - المشرقين والمغربين - اللؤلؤ والمرجان - الجلال والاكرام - السموات والأرض - الجن والانس - نار ونحاس - النواصي والأقدام - الياقوت والمرجان - نخل ورمان - رفرف خضر وعبقري حسان

In translating this sura into English translators can be classified into five categories.

1. Those who have failed to sense and therefore transfer duality and have not even attempted compensation, which results in distorted loss of the *sura*, as can be noted in the translations of Yusuf Ali and Pickthall:

- Then which of the favours of *your* Lord will *ye* deny? (Yusuf Ali: 1368)

- Which is it, of the favours of your Lord that ye deny ? (Mohammad Pickthall: 707)

By employing back-translation technique, the *aya* will be :

فبأي الآء ربك تكذب/ربكم تكذبون ؟

(The archaic personal pronoun *ye* أنتم is the plural of *thou*. أنت

2. Those who have compensated for the loss of duality by adding an indicative word such as *both*.

- So which of your Lord's blessings do *both* of you deny ? (Abdlhaqq and Aisha Bewley:527)

- So which of your Lord's bounties will *both of* you deny ? (Irving: 531)

- Which of your Lord's bounties will you and you deny? (Arberry:557)

3. Those who add a word of duality and employ exophoric reference.

- Then which of the blessings of your Lord will you both (jinn and men) deny ?) Hilali and Khan: 728)

4. Those who resort to foot-noting

- Then which of the favours 5180

Of your Lord will ye deny ?

(Footnote 5180 refers to duality and presents detailed elucidation of the sura.)

(Mushaf Al-Madinah An-Nabawaiyah)

- Which of your Lord's blessings would you[2] deny ?

(Footnote 2 : the pronoun is in the dual number, the word being addressed to mankind and the jinn. This refrain is repeated no less than 31 times) (N.J. Dawood: 19)

5. Those who add a word of duality, i.e., *both*, and provide a footnote:

- Then to whichever of your Lord's boons do you (both)[6] cry lies ? (Footnote 6 : i.e., the jinn and mankind) (Ghali: 531)

6.1.1.2. Syntactic Level

On the syntactic level , the discrepant systems of English and Arabic generate loss which necessitates compensatory strategies to aid the translator to look for functional rather than formal equivalence. Here are but two examples: **tense** and **condition**.

When tense and aspect combined together there are 12 tenses in English, some of which have no equivalents in Arabic, such as present perfect and present continuous or progressive. The Arabic past or perfective tense refers to past, present or future time. The failure to capture the exact reference to time may result in a serious semantic loss. This can be illustrated by the verb *jaa'a* جاء in the following Quranic *ayas*:

1. (وجاء السحرة فرعون) [الأعراف:113]

2. (وجاءت سكرة الموت) [ق:19]

3. (وقل <u>جاء</u> الحق وزهق الباطل) [الإسراء:81]

4. (وسيق الذين كفروا إلى جهنم زمرا حتى إذا جاءوها فتحت أبوابها) [الزُّمَر:71]

The verb *jaa'a* جاء in the above four *ayas* denotes past, present, present perfect and future tenses respectively :

1. The sorcerers **came** to Pharaoh

2. And the agony of death **comes** in truth

3. Say : Truth **has** (*now*) **come** and falsehood has vanished

4. And those who disbelieve **will be driven** in throngs to hell, till they **have come** to it , the gates thereof **will be opened**

Translators, however, differ with regard to tense and time. Instead of the present tense adopted be Arberry, Asad, among others, some think the future is meant in the second *aya* above:

- And death's agony **comes** in truth (Arberry:540)

- And (then,) the twilight of death **brings** with it the (full) truth (Asad: 798)

- And the stupor of death **will come** in truth (Hilali and Khan: 703)

The agony of death **will come** (and confront you) with truth (Irving:519)

And the stupor of death **will bring** truth (before his eyes (Yusuf Ali: 1349)

The fourth *aya* refers to the Day of Judgment or the Doomsday, where the English modals *will* and *shall* (the latter used by Arberry) explicitly express futurity, which Pickthall seems to have missed by opting for the present tense:

- And those who disbelieve **are driven** unto hell in troops till, when they reach it, and the gates thereof **are opened** .

Condition is another problematic syntactic area where loss in translation can be detected. In English, there are four kinds: real (factual), probable (likely to happen), improbable (unlikely to happen) and impossible. Each kind is determined by the verb tense or form in both the main clause (apodosis) and the subordinate clause (protasis). The conditional particles *if* and *unless* do not play any role in the determinacy of any of the above kinds. In fact, the conditional complex sentence may not contain any particle where an auxiliary verb *had*, *were* or the modal *should* introduces the dependent clause.

In Arabic, on the other hand, there are two main kinds: real or factual and improbable/impossible. Both the real and the hypothetical are determined by conditional particle: *inn* ان , *idhaa* اذا and *law* لو The first two particles in Arabic denote the first two kinds in English, whereas the third Arabic particle لو denotes the other two, and requires prefixing the main verb with *laam* ل. In the Qur'an only *inn* ان and *law* لو are used for explicit condition while *idhaa* اذا is a temporal particle, sometimes with implicit condition, equivalent to *when*.

Here are ten English translations of a Quranic *aya* wherein the first three employ verb forms indicating impossible condition which semantically contradicts the second part of it.

(ولو شاء الـلـه لذهب بسمعهم وأبصارهم إن الـلـه على كل شيء قدير (20))) [البقرة:20]

- And if Allah **had** so **decided**, He **would** indeed **have gone** away with their hearing and their beholdings. Surely, Allah is Ever Determiner over everything. (Ghali : 4)

- *Had* God **willed**, He **would have taken** away their hearing and their sight. Truly, God is powerful over everything. (Arberry : 3)

- And if Allah **willed**, He **could have taken** away their hearing and sight. Certainly, Allah has power over all things. (Hilali and Khan : 6)

The other translators have rightly opted for the improbable condition because it is not impossible for God Who is Capable to do all things, but He does not will this - that is, He does not preclude the possibility that "those who have taken error in exchange for guidance أولئك الذين أشتروا الضلالة بالهدى may one day perceive the truth and mend their ways" (cf: footnote 12 in Asad, p.6).

- If Allah **wished**, He **could take** their hearing and their sight. Allah has power over all things.

(Adalhaqq and Aisha Bewley: 4)

- And if God so **willed**, He **could** indeed **take** away their hearing and their sight: for verily, God has the power to will anything. (Asad: 6)

- If Allah **pleased**, He **could take** away their sight and hearing; He has power over all things. (Dawood: 327)

- If God **wanted**, He **would take** away their hearing and sight; God is Capable of everything. (Irving : 4)
- If Allah **willed**, He **could destroy** their hearing and their sight. Lo! Allah is Able to do all things. (*Pickthall* : 4)
- If Allah *willed*, **He could take** away their faculty of hearing and seeing; for Allah hath power over all things.

(Yusuf Ali : 20; and Musshaf Al-Madinah An-Nabawiyah)

Perhaps the **cognate object** or **accusative** المفعول المطلق poses a serious challenge for any translator from Arabic into English, simply because it is very common in the first and very rare in the second, in few instances such as: *live a life* or *dream a dream*. This object serves as an effective means for emphasis and persuasion as well as a rhetorical function of musicality. The loss is not only inevitable but also hardly compensatable. In the Glorious Qur'an, the cognate object or accusative **'adhaaban عذابا** following the verb **adhaba عذب** recurs in eleven *suras*, in two of which more that once. To compensate for this loss, the translators of the Qur'an have adopted three strategies: first, deriving the noun from the verb as in *punish* (v) and *punishment* (n), *chastise* (v) and *chastisement* (n), *torment* (v and n), thus producing unnatural rendition in English for quite natural Arabic counterpart; second, using a different noun; third, using an adverb of manner so as to be somehow natural in English. The first three of the following ten translators of the two *ayas* from *suras* Al-*Umraan* and *An-Nisaa'* seem to have adopted the first strategy, the other five the first and the second, and the last two the second and the third:

- (فأما الذين كفروا فأعذبهم عذابا شديدا) [آل عمران:56]

- (وأما الذين استنكفوا واستكبروا فيعذبهم عذابا أليما) [النساء:173]

1. Abdalhaqq and Aisha Bewley (50; and 92) :

- As for those who are kafir, I will **punish** them with a harsh **punishment**.

- As for those who show disdain and grow arrogant, He will **punish** them with a painful **punishment**.

2. Arberry (55; and 97):

-As for the unbelievers, I will **chastise** them with a terrible **chastisement** .

- and as for them who disdain, and wax proud, them He will **chastise** with a painful **chastisement**.

3. Ghali (57; and 105):

- So, as for the ones who have disbelieved, then I will **torment** them a strict **torment**

- So, as for (the ones) who disdained and waxed proud, then He will **torment** them a painful **torment**

4. Ali, Yusuf (142; and 240):

- As for those who reject faith, I will **punish** them with terrible **agony**.

- But those who are disdainful and arrogant, He will **punish** with a grievous **penalty**.

5.Asad (75; and 137):

93

- And as for those who are bent on denying the truth, I shall cause them to *suffer a suffering* severe in this world
- whereas those who felt too proud gloried in their arrogance He will **chastise** with grievous **suffering**

6. Hilali and Khan (77; and 140)
- As for those who disbelieve, I will **punish** them with a severe **torment**
- But as for those who refused His worship, He will **punish** them with a painful **punishment**

7. Mushaf Al-Madinah An-Nabawiyah (157; and 273):
- As for those who reject faith, I will **punish** them with severe **chastisement**
- But those who are disdainful and arrogant, He will **punish** them with a grievous **chastisement**

8.Pickthall (71; and 132):
-- As for those who disbelieve I shall **chastise** them with a heavy **chastisement**
- and as for those who were scornful and proud, them will He **punish** with a painful **doom**

9. Irving (57; and 105):
- As for those who disbelieve, I will **punish** them **severely**
- He will **punish** those who act scornfully and proud with painful **torment**

10. Dawood (401; and 374):
- The unbelievers shall be **sternly punished**
- As for those who are scornful and proud, He will **sternly punish** them

In *aya* 83 of *sura*t Mariam (Mary) two of the above ten translators have ventured to imitate the Arabic style and derived a cognate noun, thus producing not only unnatural English but also far from the intended meaning.

(أَلَمْ تَرَ أَنَّا أَرْسَلْنَا الشَّيَاطِينَ عَلَى الْكَافِرِينَ تَؤُزُّهُمْ أَزًّا (83)) [مريم:83]
[

Art thou not aware that We have let loose all satanic forces upon those who deny the truth – (forces) that **impel** them (towards sin) with strong **impulsion** ? (Asad : 467)

- Have you not seen that We sent Ash-Shayatins against the disbelievers, **alluring** them by (every manner of) **allurement**? (Ghali:311)

The other eight preferred loss over unacceptability:

- Do you not see that We send the shaytans against those who are kafir to **goad them on**? (Aabdalhaqq and Aisha Bewley: 292)

- Seest thou not that We have set the Evil Ones on against the Unbelievers, to **incite them with fury**? (Ali, Yusuf : 761)

Hast thou not seen how We sent the Satans against the unbelievers, to **prick them** ? (Arberry : 309)

Know that we send down to the unbelievers who **incite them to evil** (Dawood: 37)

- See you not that We have sent the shayatins (devils) against the disbelievers to **push them to do evil** ? (Hilali and Khan : 412)

- Have you not seen how We send devils to disbelievers, **to provoke them to fury?** (Irving : 311)

- Seest thou not that We have set Satans on against the unbelievers, to **incite them with fury** ?

(Mushaf Al-Madinah An-Nabawiyah : 874)

- Seest thou not that We have set the devils on the disbelievers, to **confound them with confusion** ? (Pickthall : 403)

It should be noted that all the above translators and perhaps others as well have not assimilated the semantic implication of the cognate accusative "**azzan** أزّا" which echoes the sound of the hissing steam arising from a boiling kettle, derived from the verb **yu"uzz** يؤزّ which implies seduction with hastiness and annoyance. Explicitly, they have all lost the concepts of hastiness and hissing, as evinced in At-Tonji's explication of the phrase **t"uzzuhum** تؤزّهم 'as to push them towards sins with hissing, hastiness and annoyance'.

6.1.1.3. Semantic Level

This kind of loss is very common and often inevitable in translation as it is a corollary of the lack of equivalence in English and Arabic, especially in the domain of culture-specificity: many religious and cultural words have no equivalents in the two languages such as terms of kinship. Conspicuously, the most serious loss in translation is when the meaning, be it denotative or connotative, is lost or distorted, which undermines the purpose or skopos and even the justification of translation as an act of bilingual communication. The loss is aggravated when the Qur'an, the Word of God is involved. Here are two examples of the denotative and connotative loss in the following *ayas*:

-(فإذا فرغت فانصب (7)) [الشَّرح:7]

Arberry has completely missed the intended denotative meaning, i.e., the completion of work, and has chosen an uncontextualized one, i.e., *empty*: This loss is, obviously, avertable.

- So when thou art **empty**, labour (Arberry: 649)

An example of another avertable loss in connotation is the translation of **amaani** أماني the plural of **imniyah** منية I in the following *ayas*:

-(ومنهم أميون لا يعلمون الكتاب إلا أَماني وإن هم إلا يظنون (78))

[البقرة:78]

- وقالوا لن يدخل الجنة إلا من كان هودا أو نصارى تلك أَمانيهم)

[البقرة:111]

The first *aya* refers to the Jews among whom are illiterate or unlettered people who have no real knowledge of the Old Testament, yet they depend on or trust false desires or just wishful thinking: they simply guess or speculate. Likewise, the second of the above *ayas* speaks of the Jews and Christians who think they alone will enter Paradise, which is again but false desires or no more than wishful thinking.

Obviously, the intended Quranic *meaning has a pejorative or derogatory sense*, *i.e.*, *vain or false* desires, a sort of wishful thinking. Irving, however, has mistranslated this lexical item into '*amen*' which has an appreciative connotation, because this interjection is used at the end of a prayer, invocation or hymn meaning 'so be it' or ' may it be so' as in saying 'Amen to that' meaning 'I certainly agree to that'.

- Some of them are illiterate and do not know the Book except to say '*Amen*' to it.

- They say: "No one will enter the Garden unless he is a Jew or a Christian. Those individuals are merely saying '***Amen***' (to their leaders)" (Irving : 12 and 17).

6.1.1. 4. Textual Level

Cohesion is one of the most significant constituents of the text:. It can be achieved via certain cohesive devices such as conjunctions, referring expressions, ellipsis, substitution, repetition and parallelism. Arabic and English deal with coordination and subordination in different ways: coordination is employed to express thoughts which are syntactically and semantically equal. The excessive use of coordinated, conjoined clauses in English may make the text rather boring to read and hard to focus on the ideas expressed in it, whereas subordination is deemed more elegant, and by corollary, more favoured than coordination based on parallelism which is a rhetorical device or figure of speech and a salient feature of good style in Arabic. Furthermore, the Arabic coordinators are in many cases functionally equivalent to English subordinators. The disregard of such kind of functional equivalence will result in loss of cohesion in the target text. The Arabic most recurrent coordinator **wa** الواو which recurs 157 times in *surat Yusuf* (Joseph) performing a binary task of both coordination and subordination which is not always adopted in the translations of the Qur'an , thus creating loss on the textual level as explicated below.

In *aya* 3 of the above *sura,* *wa* is equivalent to the English subordinator *though, even though* rather than the additive coordinator *and* . Four of the following ten translators have rightly opted for subordination, two for
coordination, one has lexicalized phrase , i.e., *seeing that* and three have missed it altogether :

(نَحْنُ نَقُصُّ عَلَيْكَ أَحْسَنَ الْقَصَصِ بِمَا أَوْحَيْنَا إِلَيْكَ هَذَا الْقُرْآنَ وَإِن كُنتَ مِن قَبْلِهِ لَمِنَ الْغَافِلِينَ) [يوسف:3]

We tell the best of stories in revealing this Qur'an unto thee, (O Prophet,) **even though** you were unaware of it before it came. (Abdalhaqq and Aisha Bewley: 218)

- We shall relate to thee the fairest of stories in that We have revealed to thee this Koran, **though** before it thou was one of the heedless. (Arberry : 226)

- In revealing the Koran We will recount to you the best of histories , **though** before We revealed it you were heedless of Our signs. (Dawood : 38)

- We narrate unto thee (Muhammad) the best of narratives in that We have inspired in thee this Qur'an, **though** aforetime thou wast the heedless. (Pickthall : 301-302)

- We relate unto you (Muhammad) the best of stories through Our Revelations unto you, of this Qur'an. **And** before (i.e., before the coming of Devine Revelation to you), you were among those who knew nothing about it (the Qur'an) Hilali and Khan : 304)

-We, Ever We, narrate to you the fairest of narratives in that We have revealed to you this Qur'an, **and** decidedly before it you were indeed one of the heedless. Ghali:235)

- In the measure that We reveal this Qur'an unto thee, (O Prophet,) We explain it to thee in the best possible way, **seeing that** ere this thou wert indeed among those who are unaware (of what revelation is) (Asad : 337)

- We do relate unto thee the most beautiful of stories, in that We reveal to thee this (portion of the) Qur'an: before this, thou wast among those who knew it not. (Ali, Yusuf : 546)

- We relate the best stories to you, since We have revealed this Reading to you. You were someone quite unaware previously. (Irving : 235)

- We do relate unto thee the most beautiful of stories, in that We reveal to thee this (portion of the) Qur'an: before this, thou too was among those who knew it not. (Mushaf Al-Madinah An-Nabawiyah: 623)

6.1.1.5. Stylistic/Rhetorical Level

Loss, mostly inevitable, is expected in translating a stylistically *sui generis* text such as the Qur'an, which is matchless and inimitable. The common rhetorical device metaphor is a clear case in point, where literal rendition into English may not only cause unintelligibility but also a comic response , as it can be conspicuously demonstrated in the translation of the metaphor **libaas** as *garments* of which the singular means a sort of covering, as *vestment* meaning a ceremonial garment especially one worn by a priest in church, or as *raiment* which is archaic, denoting clothing in general in the *aya* 187 in *surat Al-Baqara*. (The Cow):

- (هُنَّ لِبَاسٌ لَكُمْ وَأَنتُمْ لِبَاسٌ لَهُنَّ) [البقرة:187]

They (referring to women) are **libaas** to men, and you (men) are **libaas** to them (i.e. women).

According to At-Tabari and Ibn Kathir, among others, *libaas* means *sakan* which denotes the pleasure and comfort enjoyed by husbands living with their wives. *Aya* 189 in *surat Al-A'raaf* endorses this denotation in stating the God has created human beings from a single person, i.e. Adam, and He has created from him his wife, i.e., Eve, in order that he might enjoy the pleasure of living with her. i.e., *sakan* :

(هُـوَ الَّـذِي خَلَقَكُـم مِّـن نَّفْـسٍ وَاحِـدَةٍ وَجَعَـلَ مِنْهَـا زَوْجَهَـا لِيَسْـكُنَ إِلَيْهَـا)
[الأعراف:189]

To compensate for the inevitable loss, some translators have adopted the strategy of turning the metaphor into simile while others have rightly opted for the ground of the metaphor as is shown below.

-They are your **garments**. And ye are their **garments**.(Ali: 76)

-They are a **garment** for you, and you are a **garment** for them (Ghali : 29)

- They are **garments** for you while you are **garments** for them (Irving : 29)

- They are your **garments**. And ye are their **garments**
(Mushaf Al-Madinah Al-Nabawiyah: 77)
- They are a **vestment** for you, and you are a **vestment** for them
(Arberry : 24)
- They are **raiment** for you and ye are **raiment** for them
(Picklthall : 35)
-They are **clothing** for you and you for them (Abdalhaqq and
Aisha: Bewley : 25)
- They are **as a garment** for you, and you are **as a garment** for
them (Asad : 39)
- They are a **comfort** to you as you are to them (Dawood : 343)
Hilali and Khan (p.38) have employed a dual strategy of
transliteration and explication in which they presented one
meaning of *libas* as *sakan* quoting *aya* 189 in *surat* Al-A'araf
mentioned above.

- They are *libas* (i.e. body cover, or screen, or *Sakan* (i.e. you
enjoy the pleasure of living with them – as in 7: 189)
for you and you are the same for them.(Hilali and Khan: 38)
Likewise, the verb *ya"kul* يأكل in *aya* 275 in *surat Al-Baqara*
and *aya* 130 in *Al-Umran: ya"kulu-l-riba* has been rendered
literally as *eat, devour, gorge,* or *feed* by eight of the following ten
translators. Instead of translating the metaphor, its ground
should be rendered, i.e., take or practice *riba*. Only two seem to
have adopted a TL-oriented approach by opting for the ground.

(الَّذِينَ يَأْكُلُونَ الرِّبَا لاَ يَقُومُونَ إِلاَّ كَمَا يَقُومُ الَّذِي يَتَخَبَّطُهُ الشَّيْطَانُ مِنَ الْمَسِّ)

[البقرة:275]

(يَا أَيُّهَا الَّذِينَ آمَنُواْ لاَ تَأْكُلُواْ الرِّبَا أَضْعَافًا مُّضَاعَفَةً) [آل عمران:130]

- You who have believed, do not **eat** *riba,* doubled (and) redoubled (Ghali : 66)

- O you who believe! **Eat** not Riba (usury) doubled and multiplied (Hilali and Kan : 92)

- O believers, **devour** not usury, doubled and redoubled (Arberry : 61)

- O ye who believe! **Devour** not usury Doubled and multiplied (Ali : 161)

- O ye who believe! **Devour** not Usury Doubled and multiplied (Mushaf Al-Madinah An-Nabawiyah: 180)

- O ye who believe! **Devour** not usury, doubling and quadrupling (the sum lent) (Pickthall : 83)

- O YOU who have attained to faith! Do not **gorge** yourselves on usury, doubling and re-doubling (Asad : 87)

- You who have iman! Do not **feed** on riba, multiplied and then remultiplied (Abdalhaqq and Aisha Bewley :59)

- Believers, do not **live** on usury, doubling your wealth many times over - (Dawood : 407)

- You who believe, do not **live** off usury which is compounded over and over again (Irving : 66)

6.2.Gain

The generic differences in the two language systems naturally generate loss on all levels. Gain, on the other hand, is very rare, if ever, because, as Bassnett (2002:38) points out, translation theoreticians as well as practitioners are mainly concerned with matters of equivalence and the like, "ignoring what can also be gained, for the translator can at times enrich or clarify the SL text. Moreover, what is often seen as 'lost' from the SL context may be replaced in the TL context". By the same token, Nida and Taber (1974:106) aver that " whereas one inevitably loses many idioms in the process of translation, one can also stand to gain a number of idioms." Nida calls for some sort of compensation for the loss of a SL idiom:

> One of the difficulties is that too often translators are not sufficiently sensitive to the possibilities of idiomatic expressions, and hence the end result is a weakening of the figurative force of the translation, since they do not compensate for the loss of certain idiom by the introduction of others.

(Nida, 1964: 106)

Gain can be achieved mostly on the stylistic/rhetorical level through the following strategies, among others:

1.Adopting a TL-oriented strategy so as to reproduce a natural and original piece of literary art, implementing the principle : "the best translation is the one that does not sound as a translation" ;

2. Repudiating the formal equivalence which produces literal, wooden and unnatural translation towards a functional, dynamic one;

3. Introducing an idiom or a rhetorical device in the TT for a non-existent one in the ST . Here are some examples.

In translating the poem by Jamil bn Mu'amar or Jamil Buthayna, Nicholson likens Jamil's pure, Platonic love for Buthayna to rain, echoing Shakespeare's similitude of mercy to rain when Portia addresses Shylock to show mercy to Antonio:

The quality of mercy is not strained

It droppeth as gentle rain from heaven

سمة الرحمة لا تحدها حدود

تنزل من السماء كالمطر الودود

Nicholson has not only introduced the metaphor 'rain', the heavenly blessing and vital for the Arabs, but also some metaphors which do not exit in the original text.

النص العربي :

ودهرا تولى يا بثين يعود	الا ليت ريعان الشباب جديد
قريب واذ ما تبذلين زهيد	فنغنى كما كنا نكون وانتم
بوادي القرى اني اذن لسعيد	ألا ليت شعري هل ابيتن ليلة
تجود لنا من ودها ونجود	وهل القين فردا بثينة مرة

Oh! Might it flower anew that youthful prime

And **restore** to us, Buthayna, the bygone time

And might we again be **blest** as we wont to be

When thy folk were nigh and-

.Grudged what thou gavest me

,Shall I ever meet Buthayan alone again

Each of us, full of love, as a cloud of rain?

To counterbalance the inevitable loss in the translation of *Du'a Al-Karawan*(The Call of the Curlew) with its poetic style and highly classical and Quranic language, we have painstakingly attempted to achieve some gains by creating, for instance, an idiom or a metaphor that has no counterpart in the original.

- وهلم نذكر تلك المأساة التي شهدناها معا وعجزنا أن ندفعها أو نصرف شرها عن تلك النفس الزكية التي **أزهقت** وعن الدم البريء الذي سفك (دعاء الكروان : 10)

So that together we may evoke the tragedy to which we were witnesses , which we could not prevent happening and whose evil we could not **keep away from** that soul which was **extinguished**, and that blood which was shed.

The passive verb in Arabic "**uzhiqat أزهقت** literally means 'perish' or 'be dead', yet the translator has opted for 'extinguished' to show that that soul is a light or a flame. (p.4)

- والخطوب تنتقل بهن من قرية الى قرية ومن ضيعة الى ضيعة **يلقين بعض اللين هنا ويلقين بعض الشدة هناك** (دعاء الكروان : 16 (

- Mishaps **tossed** them from village to village, from one district to another, **here they would find tenderness, and there bitterness.** (p.8)

- أين أجد القدرة على أن أدفع يدي مع هذه الأيدي **واحرك** فمي مع هذه الأفواه ! اِنّما أنا جالسة بين هؤلاء النساء أنظر اليهن ضيقة بهن **وأتلهى** عن الجوع بهذا الخبز الرقيق (ص 34)

- Where could I find the strength to **put out** my hand amidst these hands or make my jaws **labour** like those other jaws ?

All I could do was to sit among those women, glancing at them, irritated by them, **cheating** my hunger with small, fine pieces of bread ? (26)

- وذكرت كيف انتهينا الى هذه القرية مجهودات مكدودات آخر النهار نجلس الى شجرات من التوت ساعة وبعض ساعة نستريح لا تكاد واحدة منا تتحدث الى صاحبتها بشيء حتى اذا **طال علينا الصمت وشقت علينا الراحة وثقل علينا التفكير** قالت امنا ... (ص: 23)

- I recalled how, weary and exhausted, we had arrived in this village at the **close** of the day; we had sat beneath some mulberry trees to rest for an hour or so. We scarcely spoke to one another. But as **silence lasted too long, our inactivity became** *fretful* and **thinking was too** *oppressive*, our mother said...(pp.14-15)

ثمّ **ذكرت** ذلك الخطب الذي **ألمّ** بها

Then I **brought to memory** the mishap which had utterly **crushed** her. (13)

[Prof. A. B. As-Safi]

Chapter Seven

Translation Determinacy and Indeterminacy

7.0. Translations are generally construed as products of the underlying determinacy or indeterminacy both of which squarely rest on text-types, skopos or purpose (for elaboration, see skopos theory in Chapter Three.) and the techniques or strategies. Yet, they are not absolute; they display a spectrum of high, low and zero. In maximum indeterminacy, source texts lend themselves to more than one acceptable version in the TL, whereas zero indeterminacy is tantamount determinacy wherein one version is not only acceptable but also feasible, as explicitly evinced in the translation of poetry for indeterminacy and legal texts for determinacy.

7.1. Translation Determinacy
7.1.1. Text-Type Determinacy

Determinacy of translation simply signifies that there should only be one single product in the TL. One case in point is the word-for-word translation or Dryden's metaphase where SL individual words are replaced by TL words with sometimes strict adherence to the SL word-order. But due to the linguistic and cultural discrepancies between SL and TL, such literal translations, especially of expressive or emotive texts are awkward, unnatural, unintelligible and even unreadable because literalism distorts the sense and the syntax of the original, impedes the translator's work and stifles his creativity. This is why machine translation (MT), which basically performs mere replacement or simple substitution of words in one language for words in another, has succeeded in dealing with standardized texts employing plain, formulaic language such as weather reports, government documents, and some legal texts.

Legal texts are determinately translated to ensure precise correspondence of the rights and duties in the source text and in the translation wherein only one accurate version is accepted, in both the source and target texts. The language is a very distinct variety characterized by precision, plainness and clarity. Documents like contracts or wills, for instance, are formulaic and frozen or even fossilized so that a contract or will written or translated in the wrong formula and not according to the standardized form in both languages, is not a contract or will. This holds true for the other legal texts such as agreements, certificates, government documents, insurance policies, powers of attorney and testaments among others. Here are few examples:

Lease Contract/Agreement عقد إيجار

Or: Dwelling Unit Rental Agreement عقد إيجار وحدة سكنية

This contract/agreement/ indenture made and signed this tenth day of July, 2009 between _____ as lessor, and _____ as lessee, witnesseth

تحرر هذا العقد يوم العاشر من تموز سنة 2009 بين كل من _____ مؤجر و _____ مستأجر تقرر مايلي:

That the lessor has this day leased to the lessee the premises situated in _____ to be occupied by the lessee as a residence (or insert any other purpose for which the building is leased for) and during the term commencing on the first day of July 2009, and ending on the thirtieth day of Jane 2010, upon the terms and conditions hereinafter set forth

اجر المؤجر اليوم إلى المستأجر العقار الكائن في _____ لشغله كمسكن (أو يذكر هنا أي غرض أخر(التي تبدأ من اليوم الاول من شهر تموز سنة 2009 وحتى اليوم الثلاثين من حزيران 2010 بموجب الشروط الموضحة فيما بعد...

The lessee shall pay to the lessor as rent the sum of Five Hundred Jordanian Dinars (500 JDs) payable in advance in equal monthly installments upon the first day of each and every month during the term hereof .

يدفع المستأجر إلى المؤجر على سبيل الإيجار مبلغ خمسمائة دينار أردني تدفع مقدما على دفعات شهرية متساوية في اليوم الأول من كل شهر خلال فترة العقد.

OR:

It is agreed this 20 day of July 2009 by and between:

_____(Landlord)

_____ (Tenant)

تم الاتفاق يوم 20 تموز 2009 بين كل من _____ (مالك) و _____ (مستأجر)

That Landlord hereby lets to Tenant the premises situated in _____ upon the following terms and conditions:

على أن يؤجر المالك العقار الكائن في _____ بموجب الشروط التالية:

7.1.2. Skopos Determinacy: Skopos, a Greek term, is an approach to translation developed by Vermeer (1989) to meet the growing need in the latter half of the 20th century for the translation of scientific and academic papers, instructions for use, tourist guides and some legal texts such as contracts. According to skopos theory, translation is the production of a functionally appropriate TT, based on an existing ST, and the relationship between the two texts is specified according to the skopos of the translation. The theory even proclaims that "unless the skopos of the TT is specified, translation cannot, properly speaking, be carried out at all." (Baker, 2005: 237) .

Besides, the skopos or the intended purpose of the TT sometimes determines translation methods and strategies, or in other words, the process determines the product.

7.1.3. Process Determinacy of the Product: Static vs. Dynamic in English into Arabic translation

Translation is not only determined by text-type as seen in translating legal texts, but also by the method, approach, strategy or technique which lays constraints on the translator who commits himself to adopting it. If he, for instance, opts to formal equivalence which brings about a static translation perhaps because of being incompetent or ignorant of the dynamic type which utilizes the TL potentiality as might be demonstrated in the following examples by employing an Arabic prefix :

1. He deemed the matter easy اعتبر المسألة سهلة

2. She asked him for mercy, but his heart has turned into stone.

سألته الرحمة لكن قلبه تحول الى حجر.

3. He drew water from the well.

سحب الماء من البئر

The dynamic counterparts of the above sentences employ the Arabic prefix إست which expresses request, new state or change:

1. استسهل الأمر

2. استرحمته فاستحجر قلبه

3. استسقى من البئر

By the same token, the translator employs the accusative bound morpheme or prefix *alaf* الـف التعدية to produce a dynamic rather than a static translation, e.g.,

Too much food made him sick.

Static Tr. جعله الطعام الكثير مريضا

Dynamic Tr. امرضه افراطه في الطعام

The sad news made her cry.

Or: The sad news caused her to cry.

Static Tr. جعلتها الأنباء الحزينة تبكي..

Dynamic Tr. أبكتها الأنباء الحزينة

Likewise the translator uses the Arabic verbal sentence instead of one starting with verb to be *kaana* كان or with a noun or preposition:

1. His two hands were tired .

St. Tr. كانت يداه متعبتين

Dyn. Tr. كلت يداه

2. It is difficult to understand the question.

St. Tr. من الصعب فهم السؤال

Dyn. Tr. يصعب فهم السؤال

3.   Children are afraid of dogs

St. Tr. الأطفال خائفون من الكلاب

Dyn. Tr. يخشى الأطفال الكلاب

4.   It was night, all was quiet, there was utter silence.

St. Tr. كان الوقت ليلا وكان كل شئ هادئا وكان هناك صمت تام

Dyn Tr. حل الليل وهدأ الكون وساد صمت مطبق

5.   My friend was angry then he became tongue-tied

St. Tr. كان صديقي غاضبا ثم اصبح معقود اللسان

Dyn Tr. غضب صديقي وانقعد لسانه

In the following extract from Hemingway's **A Farewell to Arms**, the renowned Arab translator, Munir Al-Baalbaki, has opted to adopt a formal equivalence, thus producing a static translation wherein he repeats the Arabic verb to be *kauna*كان seven times as an equivalent to was /were instead of a dynamic translation wherein the sentences are introduced with ordinary verbs.

ST:

The plain **was** rich with crops; there **were** many orchards of fruit trees and beyond the plain the mountains **were** brown and bare. There **was** fighting in the mountains and at night we could see the flashes from the artillery. In the dark it **was** like summer lightning, but the nights **were** cool and there **was** not the feeling of a storm coming. (**A Farewell to Arms**, by Ernest Hemingway)

A static translation determined by formal equivalence:

كان السهل غنيا بالمحاصيل. **كان** ثمة كثير من جنائن الأشجار المثمرة،
ووراء السهل **كانت** الجبال سمراء عارية، **كان** القتال دائرا في الجبال،
وخلال الليل **كان** في استطاعتنا ان نرى وميض المـدافع، و**كـان** يخيـل
للمرء، في الظلمة، وكأنه برق الصيف، ولكن الليالي **كانـت** بـاردة، ولم
نكن نستشعر أن عاصفة توشك أن تهب. (البعلبكي 7:)

A dynamic translation free from the repetition of *kaana* كان is as
follows:

سهل غني بالمحاصيل كثرت فيه جنائن الأشجار المثمرة ومـن وراءه
اسمرت الجبال وتعرت حيث دار فيها القتال. وخلال الليل اسـتطعنا
رؤية وميض المدافع بدا في الظلمة كأنه بـرق الصيف. لكن الليـالي
لطفت حرارتها ولم يساورنا احساس بأن عاصفة آتية.

A static translation determined by formal equivalence overlooks
the cognate or accusative object in the Arabic dynamic
rendition, e.g.,

1. He loved her very much
St. Tr. احبها كثيرا جدا
Dyn Tr. أحبها حبا جما
2. It was well designed
St. Tr. صممت بصورة جيدة
Dyn Tr. صممت تصميما جيدا
3. He was given a good beating
St. Tr. ضرب بشكل مبرح
Dyn Tr. ضرب ضربا مبرحا
4. They looked at him sadly/ in a sad way.
St. Tr. نظروا إليه بحزن /بطريقة حزينة
Dyn Tr. نظروا إليه نظرة حزينة
5. He shouted as usual
St. Tr. صاح كالمعتاد

115

Dyn Tr. صاح صيحته المألوفة

6. He talks like a child

St. Tr. يتحدث كالطفل

Dyn Tr. يتحدث حديث الاطفال

7. The employer treats the workers badly (or: in a bad manner).

St Tr. يعامل صاحب العمل العمال بطريقة سيئة

يعامل صاحب العمل العمال معاملة سيئة

Manifestly, a certain method, approach, technique or strategy adopted by the translator determines his/her translation (As-Safi,2007). In our English rendition of Taha Hussein's *Du'a Al-Karawan* (The Call of the Curlew, published by E.J. Brill, Leiden:1980) , we have opted for the strategy of transferring Arabic repetition into English variation. This strategy has been backed by many proponents such as Lehrer (1974: 67) who imperatively asserts: "Do not keep using the same word repeatedly, vary the lexical choices if possible". Axiomatically, variation in English helps to drift away vagueness and to get rid of the monotonous atmosphere which is likely to flare up if repetition is conserved. Here are but few illustrative instances:

كنت **أرافقها** في اللعب على ألا العب معها، و**أرافقها** إلى الكتّاب على ألا أتعلم معها، و**أرافقها** حين يأتي المعلم ليلقـى عليهـا الـدرس قبـل الغروب على ألا أتلقى الدرس معها (دعاء الكروان , ص 18).

TT:

I **was to be with her** in her play, but not play with her; **to accompany** her to the *Kuttab*, but not learn with her; **to be present with her** when her private tutor came before sunset, but not to follow her lesson (The Call of the Curlew:10).

ST:

وذكرتُ ما ألمّ بها من البؤس طـول حياتهـا مـع ذلك الـزوج المـاجن الفاجر، **ذكرتُ** ما حرق فؤادها من الغيرة، وما آذى نفسها من الذل، وما رُوّع قلبها من الخوف.

ثم **ذكرتُ** ذلك الخطب الذي ألمّ بها فهدّها هـدا حـين جاءهـا النبـأ بان زوجها قد صُرع، وبأنه قد صرع فيما لا يشرف به صريع.

ثم **ذكرتُ** هذه الآلام التي لا حد لها، والتي غمرتها كما يغمر المـاء الغريق، حين انكرتها الاسرة انكـارا، وحـين اخرجتهـا مـن القريـة ثـم نفتها مع ابنتيها من الارض.

ذكـرتُ هـذا فلـم اسـتطع ان انكـر ولا أن أجـادل، ولم ازد عـلى أن أظهرت الطاعة والاذعان. (دعاء الكروان ,ص 21).

TT:

I **recalled** the long chain of unhappy events during her existence with a vulgar, lecherous husband. I **recounted** the jealousy which had devoured her, the humiliation which had saddened her soul and the fear which had tormented her heart.

Then I **brought to memory** the mishap which had utterly crushed her when she heard the news of her husband's murder and the deplorable and shameful conditions in which he had met death.

Then I **thought over** the infinite sufferings which had submerged her like water does a drowning man when the family had disowned her, turned her out of doors and exiled her and her two daughters.

I **relived** these sad memories which did away with any possibility of refusal or discussion; I had to obey and be resigned . (The Call of the Curlew:13)

It is worth noting that Taha Hussein seems to have used the verb *dhakara* ذكر in the more common form: *tadhakar* تذكر.

ST:

أما انا فقد **انقطع** عني صوتك ايها الطائر العزيز قليلا قليلا، **وانقطع** عني صوت خالي، **وانقطعت** عني الاشـياء كلهـا (دعـاء الكـروان ,ص 67).

TT:

But your voice, beloved bird, gradually **died away** and now I can no longer hear it; my uncle's voice **does not reach** me either. I have **lost the notion of things** around me. (The Call of the Curlew: 53)

7.2. Translation Indeterminacy

By and large, translators rarely commit themselves to one particular method or strategy. More often than not, diverse methods or strategies bring about a miscellany of translations. Furthermore, there can be more than one accurate or acceptable translation of the same source text furnished by different translators or even the same translator at different times. The possibility of generating more than one translation has prompted Willard Quine (1960:in Baker,2005: 11) to propound the thesis of the indeterminacy of translation. It is based on the notion that there are always different ways one might break a sentence into words, and different ways to distribute functions among words, hence there is no unique meaning that can be assigned to words or sentences.

Quine (Ibid) unequivocally postulates that there is always a possibility that the same expression or an expression and its translation equivalent could give voice to different modes of presentation. This is in fact, the crux of the Quinean indeterminacy which, we nevertheless maintain, applies to certain, but not all, types of texts as has already been explicated in the determinacy of translation.

Translators are typically evaluated according to the extent to which they approximate maximal preservation of meaning in rendering non-literary texts, whereas they are evaluated according to the extent to which they transfer the aesthetic values and create an equivalent sense besides the preservation of the original meaning. Explicitly, the inherent subjectivity, aestheticity and the relativist construal in translation practices render literary translation, especially poetry, totally indeterminate. Indeterminacy is thus the corollary of literature, be it original or translated, as it is prone to various interpretations and different manners of aesthetic expression. This is easily manifested in the plethora of translations of celebrated works such as those by Shakespeare and the *Qur'an* which is unanimously deemed an imitable divine literary masterpiece. Here are instances of the different translations of the introductory phrase of almost all the *Qur'anic suras* except one, i.e., the *besmala* البسملة where the translators vary not only in using either the transliterated form *Allah* or the English equivalent *God*, but also in the two adjectives or epithets: الرحمن الرحيم

- All-Merciful, Most Merciful
(Abdalhaqq and Aisha Bewley)

- Most Gracious, Most Merciful

(Ali, Abdullah Yusuf), and (Mushaf Al-Madinah An-Nabawiyah)

- **The Merciful, the Compassionate)**
(Arberry and Kassub)

- **THE MOST GRACIOUS,THE DISPENSER OF GRACE**
(Asad)

- **The Compassionate, the Merciful**
(Dawood, and Maududi)

- **The All-Merciful, The Ever-Merciful**
(Ghali)

- **The Most Gracious, the Most Merciful**
(Al-Hayik and Hilali and Khan)

- **The Mercy-giving, the Most Merciful**
(Irving)

- **The Beneficent, the Merciful**
(Pickthall)

To the above renditions, we may add one more:

- **Most Compassionate, Most Merciful.**

Albeit the surfeit of the translations of the *Qur'an*, the most recent one is not likely going to bring them to a close due to indeterminacy. This is also true to loftily literary works such as the Shakespearean plays. *Merchant of Venice* is a case in point. Consider the following translations of **Salerio** talking about the Spanish ship "Andrew":

I should not see the sandy hour-glass run,
but I should think of shallows and of flats,
And see my wealthy Andrew dock'd in sand,
Veiling her high top lower than her ribs

To kiss her burial. (I.1.25-29)

Khalil Mutran:

وإذا نظرت إلى تناقص المزولة، خطرت على بالي الجروف والأغوار الرملية وبدت لوهمي تلك الجارية الكبرى المسماة "بسنت أندري" جانحة وقد انقلب ساريتها الوسطى إلى ما تحت غاطسها كأنها تقبّل رمسها .

khtar Al-Wakil:

وإذا نظرت إلى الساعة الرملية تـذكرت المياه الضحلة والسهول الرملية وتخيلت سفينتي "اندرو" ذات الحمولة الثمينة وقد جنحت فوق الرمال وهبط صاريها العالي إلى ما دو ن غاطسها لكي تُقبّل قبرها.

Hussein Amin:

فـان نظرت إلى الرّمـل يجـري في الساعة الرملية، فكرتُ في المياه الضحلة، وتصورت سفينتي المحملة- كالسفينة -اندرو- بثمين البضائع، وقد غرّست في الرمال، وانحنى صاريها العالي إلى ما دون أضلاعها لتُقبّل قبرها.

Mohammed Anani:

وإذا نظرت عيني للساعات الرملية
خاف فؤادي قاع البحر الرملي الغادر
ورأيت السفن الكبرى جانحة فيه
وذؤابة رأس السارية تُقبّل ارض القبر.

Amer Buheiri

عة تمشي في حذار	اتراني ارقبُ السا
"اندرو" دون انتضار	بل اراعي سوقة
ع لـتقبيـل القـرار	مـال صاريها الى القا

Another example:

Jessica:

But love is blind, and lovers cannot see

121

The pretty follies that themselves commit,
For if they could, Cupid himself would blush
To see me thus transformed to a boy. (II.6.36)

Mutran (1973:74):

إنما الغرام أعمى، وليس للمتحابين أن يـرواهم آثار جنـونهم، إذ لـو
قدروا على استجلاء الحقيقة لخجل الغرام نفسـه مـن تشكّلي بهـذا
الشكل.

Al-Wakil (1983:56):

بيـد أن الحـبّ أعمـى، ولا يسـتطيع المحبـون أن يـدركوا شـيئا عـن
الحماقات اللطيفة التي يرتكبونها، لأنهم لو استطاعوا ذلك لاستحيا
كيوبيد نفسه إذا شاهدني وقد صرت غلا ما.

Amin (1990:60):

غير ان الحب اعمى والمحبون عاجزون عن رؤية الحماقات الجميلـة
التي يرتكبونها. ولو انهم كانوا مبصرين لتملك كيوبيد نفسه الخجـل
اذ يراني وقد تحولت هكذا الى غلام.

Anani (1988:97):

لكنّ الحبّ كفيف البصر
ولا يبصر اهل الحب احابيل الحب البلهاء
ان كان لربّ الحب عيون
لاستنكر ابدال ثيابي بثياب غلام

Buheiri (1978:163):

وســـره لا يـــذاع	لكنما الحبّ أعمى
وجههُ مـا استطـاع	هذا كيوبيد يحمرّ
الصبي، والأمر شاع!	إذا رآني بثوب

Poetry is perhaps the most potential domain for the
indeterminacy of translation. Not only different translators render
a poem or a stanza differently, but one translator may produce, at
different times, divergent versions. We can verifiy the above

postulation by translating and retranslating certain stanzas after
a lapse of time, as explicated below.

    So much do I love wandering
    So much I love the sea and sky
    That it will be a piteous thing
    In one small grave to lie. (Z.Akins)

(1)

كـــم أحـــب التجـــوال
وكم أحب البحر والسماء
ولعمري هو شيء مرير
أن ارقد في قبر صغير

(2)

كـــم عشقــت السفـــر
وعشقت السماء والبحر
فيا لـــه من أمـــر مـرير
أن ارقد في قبر صغير

(3)

شــــديد هو حبـــي لـــلأسفـــار
وحبـــي للسمـــاء والبحـــار
فيا للأسى أن ينتهي بي المصير
إلــى الـــرقود في قبر صغيـــر

(4)

ومتيم بالبحـر والسمـــاء   خـــليلي إني متيم بـالطواف
إلى حفرة صغيرة ظلماء   بيد إني واحسرتاه سأمضي

Another example:

Call no man a foe, but never love a stranger,
Build up no plan, nor any star pursue,
Go forth with crowds, in loneliness is danger.

(Stella Benson)

In a reverse direction of translation, we can furnish two versions of Michael Nu'aima's ميخائيـل نعيمـة beautiful poem, addressing the sea:

وفـي هياجك ذعـر؟	أفـي سكونك أمـــنُ
وفي أنقباضك عسر؟	أفــي امتـدادك يُسر
وفي ارتفاعك فخر؟	وفـي انخفاضكَ ذلّ
وفي هديرك يُسر؟	وفـي سكونكَ حُزنٌ
هل فيك خيرٌ وشرُ؟	يـا بحر يـا بحر قل لي
والبحر كــر وفـر	وقفـت والليـل داج
ولـــم يجبني بـــر	فلـم يُجبني بحـر
وكحل الأفـق فجر	وعندما شـابَ ليلـي
والكـون طيّ ونشر	سمعت نهــراً يغنــي
في البحر مدّ وجزر	في الناس خيـر وشـرٌ

Version 1

Is there security in your serenity?
Panic in your rage?
Is there relief in your stretching ?
Or distress in your shrinking?
Is there humility in your dropping?
Glory in your rising?
Sadness in your silence?
Or happiness in your surging;
O sea! Do tell me
Good and evil in thee?
The night was dark,
The sea is in retreat and attack,
I was standing, for an answer waiting,
But the sea did not tell me.
Nor did the land.

And when my night hoary turned,
And dawn the horizon darkened,
A song was the river chanting
And the world pleating and spreading
In people you find good and evil,
In sea, there is rising and ebbing.

Version 2

In your stillness, is there safety?
And fright in your fury?
In your stretch, is there facility?
And in your contraction, difficulty?
In your subsidence, is there humility?
And pride in your tide?
In your tranquility, is there sadness?
And in your surge, easiness?
O sea! O sea! Please tell me:
Is there good and evil in thee?
I stood at a night, dark and dusky,
In attack and retreat was the sea.
The sea never replied,
Nor did the land,
And when my night turned grey,
To the horizon, Dawn made its way,
I Heard a river singing.
The Universe folding and unfolding,
 Good and evil in people you see...
As ebb and tide in the sea.

There can be as many prose translations of the above stanzas as the poetic ones, due to the indeterminate nature of this kind of translation which is like painting, both being facets of art, governed by subjectivity and aestheticity, wherein different painters or even the same painter may produce different paintings of the same landscape.

Chapter Eight

Lexicalization and Modalization in English-Arabic Translation: Prepositions As a Case Study[•]

8.0. The task of the translator is multiple: as a decoder, appreciator, critic, encoder and creator who maintains an equilibrium to transfer the SL text semantically as well as stylistically. By necessity, he reads each word and each sentence in the SL text as carefully as a critic before he transfers and finally composes it in the TL. Such a transference and composition can never be achieved through literal, i.e., word-for-word translation which, Nida and Reybum (1981) rightly maintain, will inevitably tend to distort the meaning of the SL message or as Andre Lefevere (cited in Bassnett, 1996: 81) puts it, distorts the sense and the syntax of the original. Such a translation impedes the translator's work and stifles his creativity which is a manifestation of his competence and intelligence.

There is nothing new in repudiating literalism in translation, on which there is now almost a general consensus. Lefevere quotes Horace as antedating such an attitude:

> Word-for-word   translation   do
> not   find   mercy   in   our   eyes,
> not because they are against the law

[•]Published in: **IJAES: International Journal of Arabic-English Studies.** Vol. 2, Nos. 1&2.

of translation (as an act of communication) but simply because two languages are never identical in their vocabulary. Ideas are common to the understanding of all men but words and manners of speech are particular to different nations. (Bracketing is Lefevere's). (ibid)

By corollary, a SL preposition need not always be replaced literally by its formal TL equivalent, i.e., a TL preposition; rather it may well be lexicalized or modalized, i.e., replaced by a modal (auxiliary) verb or a lexical item(s), as illustrated in the following diagram:

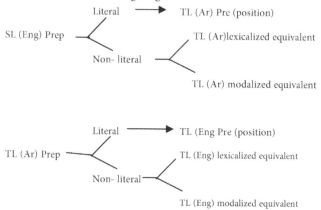

Figure 6: Translation Strategies for Lexicalization and Modalization of English Arabic prepositions.

8.1. Lexicalization:

To lexicalize a notion, according to Quirk, et al. (1985: 1526) is "in lay terms, we now have a word for it." By the same token, to lexicalize a SL preposition is to have a lexical item, a content word, as an 'equivalent' or more accurately as a 'correspondent' in the TL. Lexicalization, be it optional or obligatory, renders the meaning of an expression more explicit, or as Lyons elucidates: "it is perhaps only when semantic distinctions are lexicalized, rather than grammaticalized, that what is expressed is explicit." (Lyons, 1995:193).

8.2. Modalization

Analogous to lexicalization, modalization simply refers to the use of a TL form of modality for a SL preposition. Obviously, modality can be expressed by different parts of speech. The verbal forms of modality in English include auxiliaries such as **will, would, can, could, may, might, must, ought to, need** as well as finites such as **allow, permit** etc. In Arabic too, the verbal forms of modality include auxiliaries such as verbs of "proximation and commencement" افعـال المقاربـة والشروع like **kaada** كـاد, **awshaka** أوشـك, **shara'a** شرع, **ja'ala** جعـل **akhadha** أخذ, **qaama** قـام,P1.9, as well as finites such as **yajuuzu** يجوز, **yastatii'u** (may) يستطيع (be able to, can) etc.

The non-verbal forms of modality in English include adjectives such as **probable, possible, certain,** adverbs such as **probably, ertainly;** and nouns such as

probability, possibility, certainty in clauses such as "it is probable/ possible" or a probability/ possibility, or "it is certain! a certainty". In Arabic, too, it can be realized by adverbs such as **abadan** أبداً(absolutely) particles such as **qad** قد (may) or **qat** قـط (never) or a preposition such **ala** على or **llaam** اللام The following diagram displays modality in English and Arabic.

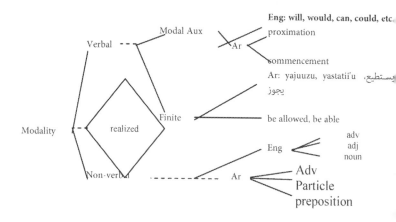

Figure 7 : Realization of the Two Kinds of Modality.

8.2.1. Modality and Modulation:

Modality is defined by Quirk, et al (1985 :219), "as the manner in which the meaning of a clause is qualified ." " The system of modality, according to Bell (1991: 139), is an extremely important one, since it gives the communicator the options of expressing an opinion about the extent to which the assertion is possible, probable, certain or frequent. He distinguishes between modality and modulation as follows: the former is concerned with propositions, the latter with proposals; the former comprises probability, possibility, certainty and frequency, the latter obligation and inclination (ibid: 139-140). Halliday (1976:209), too, distinguishes between modality and modulation but states simultaneously that" they are closely interrelated.. .. They are the same system in different functions, where 'functions' refer to components of the linguistic system: the one is interpersonal, the other ideational. Furthermore, "modulation is a condition imposed by someone; and if that someone is the speaker himself then it becomes a kind of modality" (ibid). Hence, due to this overlap and what Halliday accurately describes as " the complex nature of the relationship between modality and modulation which he considers a kind of 'quasi- modality' (ibid: 205213) it would suffice here to adopt the term 'modality as subsuming modulation.

8.3. Exemplification
8.3.1. English Modal Auxiliaries
a. You **may** be right. (Possibility: it can also be realized
   non-verbally:
a.1. It is possible that you are right.
a.2. Perhaps /Possibly, you are right.
b. **Can** you call back tomorrow? (Ability: are you able to...?)
c. You **must** be joking. (Necessity: it is necessarily the case that you are joking.
d. You **can** /**may** do as you wish. (permission: you are allowed..)

e. You **must** be back by ten o'clock. (Obligation: you are obliged to be back by ten).

-f. I'**ll** write as soon as I can. (Volition! intention: I tend to write as soon as I can).

g. I'**ll** do it, if you like. (Volition! willingness: I'm willing to do it.)

h. She **will/would** keep interrupting me. (Volition! insistence: she insists on interrupting me).

i. The guests **will/would** have arrived by that time. (prediction: they are expected to. . .)

Sometimes a modal auxiliary verb expresses more that one modal concept. The following are some examples borrowed from Quirk, et. al (1985: 219-239).

j. You **may have to**-play it again. (possibility+ obligation).

k. She **must** have been willing to help. (necessity + volition).

8.3.2. Arabic Modal Auxiliaries

The salient Arabic modal auxiliaries which precede the finite (imperfect) verbs are the verbs of proximation and commencement stated above. Here are some examples.

- *Kaada yamuutu atashan.* كاد يموت عطشاً

    (He was about to/on the point (verge) of dying of thirst).

- *Yakaadu al-barqu yakhtfu 'absaarahum*:

    (يكاد البرق يخطف أبصارهم) [البقرة:20]

    (Lightning almost snatches away their sight).

- *Shara'a ash-shaa'iru yanshidu qasiidatahu.*

شرع الشاعر ينشد قصيدته.

(The poet started/ commenced reciting his poem).

- *Akhadha yaqra'u bisautin ?aalin...* أخذ يقرأ بصوت عالٍ

(He began to read aloud.)

8.3.3. Finite Verbs of Modality

Modality can be lexicalized by finite verbs such as yajuuzu, yastatii'u (may/ might, can/ could), or verbs like allow:

- *Tastatii? ann taf?al maa tashaa'* تستطيع أن تفعل ما تشاء

(You can / may do as you wish)

- *Yaiuuzu/ yasmahu laka ann tudakhin.* يجـوز (يسـمح لـك) أن
تدخن

(you can/ are allowed to smoke),

- *yuhtamal! vuraiahu ann yusaafira ghadan.*

يحتمل/ يرجح أن يسافر غداً

(It is probable that he will travel tomorrow)

8.3.4. Non-verbal Modality

The bracketed sentences above exemplify non-verbal modality in English. In Arabic it can be realized by a noun, a particle or a preposition as mentioned above and as illustrated in the examples below.

8.4. Rendition of English Prepositions into Arabic: The Strategy of Lexicalization

By employing the above strategy, English prepositions are lexicalized instead of being replaced literally by Arabic equivalent prepositions.

The strategy is hoped to reproduce a vivid, creative and dynamically communicative translation. In the following examples, some Arabic lexical items are bracketed to indicate optionality; otherwise lexicalization is obligatory.

8.4.1. after

- She was named <u>after</u> her mother. سميت باسم أمها

8.4.2. at

- The country has been <u>*at*</u> war with the neighbour for eight years
كان البلد في (حالة) حرب مع جارتها لمدة ثمانية أعوام.

8.4.3. before

- He stood <u>*before*</u> the king. مثل (في حضرة) الملك

- The ship sailed <u>*before*</u> the wind (with the flowing wind from behind)
أبحرت السفينة باتجاه الريح

8.4.4. behind

- She is <u>*behind*</u> her brother in work.

إنها (مختلفة) عن أخيها في العمل

8.4.5. below

- It is <u>*below*</u> your dignity to do that. لا يليق بك أن تفعل ذلك

8.4.6. down

- There is an exhibition of costumes <u>*down*</u> the ages.

هناك معرض للأزياء يغطي العصور كافة.

8.4.7. for

- They fight <u>*for*</u> their country يقاتلون دفاعاً عن/ في سبيل / بلدهم
- His lawyer acts <u>*for*</u> him in this case.

يعمل محاميه نيابة عنه في هذه القضية

- The university gave a dinner *for* him .

قدمت الجامعة غداء تكريماً له

8.4.8. in

- Glory *in* the mist مجد يكتنفه الضباب
- The woman *in* black المرأة المتشحة بالسواد .

8.4.9. of

- Mr. Jones, *of* the Manor farm, had locked the hen-houses. (Orwell: *Animal Farm*)

أغلق السيد جونز صاحب حقل مانور بيوت الزجاج.

8.4.10. on

- There are some evidences *on* her.

هناك بعض الأدلة في غير صالحها/ ضدها

8.4.11. over

- He will stay *over* the weekend.

سيمكث حتى نهاية (طيلة) عطلة الآسبوع

- *Over* the entire country. على طول البلاد وعرضها

8.4.12. to

- She sang *to* her guitar غنت بمصاحبة قيثارها.

8.5. Rendition of Arabic Prepositions into English

8.5.1. Strategy of Lexicalization

It is perhaps worth reiterating that this strategy is based on a functional equivalence and on a hermeneutic/manipulative approach. Here are some examples.

8.51.1. bi الباء

- *Laysa biya ann azraka* ليس بيّ أن أضرك.

   It is not my intention to harm you.

- *al-ghurmu bi-l-ghunmi* الغُرْم بالغنم

 Gain **entails** loss. (a jurisprudential maxim)

8.5.1.2. fii في

- *Kalaamun fii kalaam* كلام في كلام

  Just (so many) words.

- *Nahnu 'aqaribun fii 'aqqrib* نحن أقارب في أقارب

  Our social relations are those of kinsfolk.

8.5.1.3. ?ala على

- *Kaana ?ala haqq* كان على حق (He was right).

- *Huwa ?ala shi'in mina 'l-dhakaa'* هو على شئ من الذكاء
  (He has a good deal of intelligence).

- *?alayka bi'l sabr* عليك بالصبر (You must have patience or: You mus be patient.)

- *qiila ?ala lisaanihi* قبل على لسانه (He was supposed to have said)

8.5.4. ?ann عن

- *qutuluu ?ann 'aakhirihum* قتلوا عن آخرهم
  (They were killed to the last man)

- *maata ?ann tarikatin kabiira.* مات عن تركة كبيرة
  (He died leaving a large fortune).

- *?ann'bi hurayra* عن أبي هريرة (on the authority of)

8.5.5. min من

- *'akala min 'l ta?aam* أكل من الطعام (He ate some food.)

- *khudh min 'l daraahim* خذ من الدراهم (Take some money.)

- *maa lilaahi min shariik* ما لله من شريك. (God has no partner.)

8.5.6. ma'a مع

hal ma?aka qaamuus? هل معك قاموس (Have you got a dictionary?

8.6. Strategy of Modalization

- Arabic modality can also be expressed by prepositions such as
?ala على and la اللام.

8.6.1. ?ala على

As a modal, the preposition ?ala على is sometimes preceded by a
modal verb yajib يجب which is deletable.

- *Yajib ?alayka ?ann tutii'a 'l- qwaniin*

ـ (يجب) عليك أن تطيع القوانين).

(You must obey the laws.)

- *Maa ?ala ' -rasuuli 'ilaa 'l-balaagh al-mubiin.*

(ما على الرسول إلا البلاغ) [المائدة:99]

- (The messenger's duty is but to proclaim the message.)

In legal discourse, this modalized preposition denotes
commitment, equivalent to the modal **shall**:

على المطبوعات احترام الحقيقة والامتناع عن نشر ما يتعارض مع
مبادئ الحرية والمسؤولية الوطنية وحقوق الانسان وقيم الامة
العربية والاسلامية. (من قانون المطبوعات)

Publications **shall** respect truth and **shall** refrain from publishing
anything that contradicts the principles of freedom, national
obligations, human rights and values of Arab and Islamic nation.

8.6.2. (llam اللام for permission, possibility and assertion)

- laka maa tashaa'

(you can/ may do as you wish) لك ما تشاء

_llyuiziihum allaahu 'ahsana maa ?amaluu

(ليجزيهم الـله أحسن ما عملوا) [النور:38]

(God may reward them according to the best of their deeds).

- wa 'anna rabaka lahuwa_al'aziizu At- rahiim.

(وإن ربك لهو العزيز الرحيم (191)) [الشعراء:191]

(And verily your Lord is Exalted in Might, Most Merciful.)

- la' ann 'amartahum liyukhrijanna

(لئن أمرتهم ليخرجن) [النور:53]

(If you command them, they *would* leave their homes.)

8.6.3. The strategy explained above can be reversed in directionality, so that English modality can be realized by prepositions in Arabic. Some examples in 8.6 above evince that some English modals can be rendered into modalized prepositions in Arabic:

- Can you call back tomorrow? هل لك أن تتصل ثانية غداً؟
- You must be back by ten o'clock.

(يجب) عليك أن تعود بحلول الساعة العاشرة

- She will/would keep interrupting me.

إنها لتقاطعني باستمرار/ إنها تصر على مقاطعتي

- The guest may/ might/ will/ would! have arrived by that time.

ربما يكون الضيوف قد وصلوا في ذلك الوقت.

- You may have to play it again. ربما يتحتم عليك أن تلعب ثانية.
- She must have been willing to help.

لا بد أنها كانت راغبة في المساعدة.

By way of conclusion, to be dynamically communicative and effective, translation as a TL product should be as semantically accurate, grammatically correct, stylistically adequate and textually coherent as the ST. Such a product can never be realized through the so-called literal or word-for-word approach, but rather through a creativity-oriented, hermeneutic /manipulative one which has prompted two strategies for the rendition of English/Arabic prepositions. The first strategy is that of lexicalization, the second of modalization; through the former, the SL prepositions are lexicalized in the TL, through the latter they are modalized whether verbally or non-verbally. The manipulation of the two strategies require a rather exceptional translation competence which capacitates the translator to perform a multiple task: as a ST decoder/appreciator or a critic and as a TT encoder/creator who caters not only for the transference of the semantic values but of the aesthetic values as well. Exemplification has verified the two strategies which serve to produce an accurate, vivid, creative and effective translation.

References

- Abdulhaqq and Aisha Bewley. 1999. **The Noble Qur'an.** Norwich (UK): Bookwork.

 - Adams, Robert M. 1973. **Proteus; His lies, His truth: Discussions of Literary Translation.** New York: North & Company Inc.

- Al-Hayik, Iz-zu Din. 1996. **A Simplified, Clear and Approximate Translation of the Meanings of the Holy Koran into English.** Damascus: Dar Al-Fikr for Publishing.

- Ali, Abdullah Yusuf. 1989. **The Meaning of the Holy Qur'an.** Brentwood (USA) Amman Corporation.

- Arberry, Arthur J . 1964. **The Koran Interpreted.** London: Oxford University Press.

- Asad, Muhammad. 1980. **The Message of the Qur'an.** Gibraltar: Dar Al-Andalus.

- As- Safi, A.B. (trans).1980. **Taha Husain. The call_of the Curlew.** Leiden: E.J.Bril.

 - As- Safi, A.B. 1994. "The Dynamic vs. Static Transation of Literary Texts from English into Arabic". **Turjuman.** Vol.3, No.1.,pp. 57-79.

 - As-Safi, A.B. 1996. "Toward an Objective Assessment of Literary/Belletrisitric Translation". **Translatio.** Vol XV, No.1, pp. 5-20.

- As-Safi, Abdul-baki and As-Sharifi, In'am Sahib. 1997. "Naturalness in Literary Translation". **Babel.** Vol.43, No.1. pp 60-75.

- As-Safi, A.B. 2001. "Modalization and Lexicalization of Prepositions in English-Arabic Translation." **IJAES: International Journal of Arabic-English Studies.** Vol. 2, Nos. 1&2.

- As-Safi A.B. 2004. " Machine Translation: Reality and Aspirations:. In **Conference on Language and Translation: Proceedings of the 2**[nd] **International**

الصافي، عبد الباقي . " الترجمة الآلية : الواقع والتطلعات". مؤتمر أطلس الدولي
الثاني في اللفة والترجمة: دور التكنولوجية الحديثة في تعليم الغات وتعلمها. عمان:
2004، ص:207-227 .

- As-Safi, Abdul Baki. 2006. "Translation of Arabic Literary Works: Taha Hussein's Du'a Al-Karawan (The Call of the Curlew: A Case Study". In **Atlas for Studies and Research**. Vol. 1., No. 1.

- As-Safi, A.B. 2007. "Theories, Methods and Strategies of Translation". **Atlas Global Center for Studies and Research**. Vol. 2, No. 1, pp. 15-22.

- Bahumayd, S.A. 1995. "On the teaching of Translation at the Univeristy Level". **Turjuman**. Vol. 4, No.2.

- Baker, Mona. 1992. **In Other Words: A Coursebook on Translation**. London: Rouytledge.

- Baker, Mona.(ed). 2005. **Routledge Encyclopedia of Translation Studies**. London: Routledge.

- Bassnett, Susan.1988. **Translation Studies.** 3rd Ed. London: Routledge.

--------------. (1996) **Translation studies**. Revised Edition. London: Routledge.

- Bell, Roger T.1991. **Translation and Translaling: Theory and Practice**. London and New York: Longman.

- Catford, J.C. 1965. **A Linguistic Theory of Translation**. London: Oxford University Press.

-Chesterman, Andrew (ed.).1989. **Readings in Translation Theory**. Helsinki: Oy Finn Lectura Ab.

- Dawood, N.J. 1994. **The Koran**. London: Penguin Books.

- El-Shiyab, R. and R. Hussein. (2000). "On the Use of Compensatory Strategies in Simultaneous Interpretation".

META: Vol XIV, No3, 2000. Montreal: La Press de l'Unversité de Montreal, pp. 548 – 557.

- Emery, Peter G. 2000. "Introduction to Translation theory and Contrastive Textology in Arab University Translation Classes." **IJAES: International Journal of Arabic-English Studies.** Vol.1, No.1,

- Ghali, Muhammad Mahmud. 2002. **Towards Understanding the Ever-Glorious Qur'an.** Cairo: Dar An-Nashr Lilijami'at.

- Halliday, M.A.K. (1976). "Modality and Modulation in English". In Gunther Kress, (ed.), **Halliday: System and Function in Language.** London: Oxford University Press.

- Hemingway, Ernest. 1995. **A Farewell to Arms.** Beirut: Libraire du Liban, p.3.

Graham, Joseph F. 1981. "Theory for Translation" in Rose (ed) below.

- Gutt, Ernst-August. 2000. **Translation and Relevance: Cognition and Context.** Manchester & Boston: St. Jerome Publishing.

- Hervey, Sandor and Higgins, Ian. 1992. **Thinking Translation : A Course in Translation Method: French-English.** London: Routledge,p.35.

- Hilali, Muhammad Taqi-ud-Din and Khan, Muhammad Muhsin. 1984. **The Noble Qur'an.** Madinah: King Fahd Complex for the Printing of the Holy Qur'an.

- Hussein, Taha. 1980. **The Call of the Curlew.** Translated by As-Safi. Leiden: E.J.Brill.

- Irving, Thomas. 1992. **The Noble Qur'an.** Brattleboro (USA): Amana Books.

- Jackendoff, Ray. (1972). **Semantic Interpretation in Generative Grammar.** Cambridge, Massachusetts: MIT

Press. Pp. 400, p – in Nicholson, Nancy S, (1991). "Linguistic Theory and Simultaneous Interpretation: Semantic and Pragmatic Considerations". **Babel**, Vol 37, No 3, P. 96

- Koller, Werner. 1989. "Equivalence in Translation theory". In Chesterman, ed., **Op.Cit.**

- Kassab, Rashid. 1994.**The Translation of the Meanings of the Qur'an.** Amman: Kilani and Sakkur Publishing.

- Jakobson, Roman. 1959. "On Linguistic Aspects of Translation." In **On Translation.** Cambridge, Mass: Harvard University Press.

- Larson, Milded L. 1998. **Meaning-Based Translation: A guide to Cross-Language Equivalence.** New York: University Press of America.

- Lefevere, Andre'. (1992). **Translation: History and Culture.** London: Routledge

- Lehrer, Adrienns. 1974. **Semantic Fields and Lexical Structures.** Amsterdam & London: North-Holland Publishing Co.

- Lyons, John. (1995). **Linguistic Semantics.** Cambridge: Cambridge University Press.

- Ouirk, Randolph, Sidney Greenbaun, Geoffery Leech and Jan Savrtvik. 1985. A **Comprehensive Grammar of the English Language.** London: Longman.

- Maududi, Abu Al'aa. **The Holy Qur'an.** Lahor: Islamic Publications.

- Munday, Jeremy. 2001. **Introducing Translational Studies: Theories and Applications.** London: ROutledge.

-Newmark, Peter.1981. *Approaches to Translation.* Oxford: Pergamon Press .

- Nida, Engene A. 1964. **Toward a Science of Translating**. Leiden. E.J. Brill, pp. 1-2, 82.

- Nida, E and Taber, C. 1969. **The Theory and Practice of Translation**. Leiden: E.J. Brill.

-. Nida, Eugene A.1976. "A Framework for the Analysis and Evaluation of Theories of Translation". In R.W. Brislin .(ed). **Translation: Applications and Research**. New York: Gardner Press, pp. 47-79.

- Nida, E. and Reybum, W.D. 1981. **Meaning across Cultures**. New York: Orbis Books.

- Nord, Christiane. 2007. **Translating as a Purposeful Activity: Functionalist Approafches Explained**. Manchester: St. Jerome Publishing.

- Palumbo, Giuseppe. 2009. **Key Terms in Translation Studies**. London: Continuum.

- Pickthall, Muhammad M. 1976. **The Glorious Koran**. London: George Allen and Unwin.

- Quah, W.V.O. 1960. **Translation and Technology**. New York: Palgrave Macmillan.

- Reiss, Katherina. 1977. "Text-types, Translation Types and Translation Assessment". In Chesterman, Andrew. Ed. **Readings in Translation Theory**. Finland: Oy Finn Lectura.Ab.

- Rose, Marilyn Gaddis. (ed). 1981. **Translation Spectrum: Essays in Theory and Practice**. Albany: State University of New York Press.

- Sager, Juan. 1994. **Language Engineering and Translation: Consequences of Automation**. Amsterdam & Philadelphia : John Benjamins Publishing Company.

- Shakespeare, W .2001. **The Merchant of Venice**. Beirut: York Press (Libraire du Liban).

- Schulte, Rainer and Biguenet, John. 1992. **Theories of Translation**. Chicago: The University of Chicago Press.

145

- Snell-Hornby, Mary. 1988. **Translation Studies: An Integrated Approach.** Amesterdam and Philadelphia: John Benjamins Publishing Company.

-Shuttleworth, Mark and Moiro Cowie. 2007. **Dictionary of Translation Studies.** Manchester: St. Jerome Publishing.

-Steiner, George. 1975. **After Babel.** London: Oxford University Press.

- Vermeer, Hans J. 1989. "Skopos and Commission in Translational Action". In Chesterman. **Op.Cit** .

Wehr, Hans. (1976). **Dictionary of Modern Written Arabic.** New York: Spoken Language Services

- Wilss, Wolfram. 1996. **Knowledge and Skills in Translator Behaviour.** Amsterdam: John Benjamins.

- Wright, W. (1996). A **Grammar of the Arabic Language.** Beirut: Librairie du Liban.

- امين ، حسين أحمد.1994.(مترجم) **تاجر البندقية.** القاهرة: دار الشروق.

- بحيري، عامر محمد. 1978. (مترجم). **مسرحيتا شكسبير (العاصفة-تاجر البندقية)** القاهرة الهيئة المصرية العامة للكتاب. ص193-194. وانظر كذلك العمر ، المصدر اعلاه، ص73.

- البعلبكي , منير. (مترجم). **ارنست همنغواي . وداعا للسلاح .** بيروت: دار العلم للملايين, 1981 .

- حسن، عباس. (1973). **النحو الوافي.** ج4، ط4، القاهرة: دار المعارف بمصر، ص 131.

- عناني، محمد.1988.(مترجم) **تاجر البندقية.** القاهرة: هيئة الكتاب . اعتمدنا في هذه الترجمة وغيرها على المصدر الآتي:

- Al-Omar, Muhammad KhairHussein.2005. **Assessment of Anani's Translation of Shakespeare's The Merchant of Venice: A Cultural Perspective.** Unpublished M.A. thesis. Yarmouk University, Jordan, pp.48-49.

- مطران، خليل.1973.(مترجم). **تاجر البندقية.** القاهرة: دار المعارف

- الوكيل، مختار. 1983.(مترجم) **تاجر البندقية.** بيروت: المركز العربي للثقافة والعلوم، ص 102-103.

Printed in the United States
By Bookmasters